# More The Same Than Different

## What I Wish People Knew About Respecting and Including People with Disabilities

by

# Lorraine Cannistra

# Table of Contents

*Dedicated to Bill Vogler, who has always accepted me exactly as I am.*

## Acknowledgements

I don't trust myself to have remembered everyone. Countless people have supported this effort in a variety of ways. I sincerely appreciate each and every one of you.

To my family far and wide—Thank you for all your encouragement.

Beth Jessop—Thank you for believing in me from start to finish.

Terrill Thomson—Thank you for reading a draft and providing thoughtful, insightful feedback. You helped me to explore the tough questions that made this book infinitely better.

Paige Lytle—An editor who makes amazing suggestions. I am so lucky to have found you.

Brenda Crawshaw—Chapter by chapter you kept it real, and always offered insight I had not previously considered.

Dale Lukert—We met on my second day of classes at ESU, and you have been looking out for me ever since. After more than 30 years of friendship, I am proud to consider you family.

Brandon White—Thank you for helping me dance in many areas of my life. And reading a draft of this book too. Love you, bro!

Michael Mintz—Thanks for encouraging me to write when I had lots of time on my hands.

Andrea Babbit—You have made my life richer in so many ways, simply by being you. "Thanks" just doesn't cover it.

Jodi and Kevin Bowersox—You went above and beyond in more ways than I can count. Saying thank you will never be enough. I sincerely appreciate all your efforts. This book would not be a reality without you.

Current and former caregivers—Thanks for all you do for me. I could not live the life I love without the assistance all of you provide. I am beyond grateful.

## Foreword

I first met Lorraine during my freshman year at the University of Kansas just as I was beginning my journey toward becoming a Physical Therapist. A friend and mentor, who was a former caregiver of Lorraine's, knew she was hiring and suggested I apply. I mean, who wouldnt wanna wear sweats, as the flyer advertising her caregiving position suggested? Little did I know just how much this experience would shape the person I am and how I view and interact with people around me.

Over the next year and a half, I learned so many things from Lorraine, like how to use people first language and how much the words we use matter. I learned about the importance of having conversations at eye-level, and I learned to always address someone directly, even if their family member, caregiver, or service dog is with them. Taken all together, these lessons show that regardless of situation, medical diagnosis, or physical ability, there are basic human interactions we can be mindful of and practice that ensure that every person feels respected, dignified, and cared for.

The lesson that I learned from Lorraine that has impacted me the most is this: to practice empathy with every interaction. We all have unique experiences, but we can always try to understand each other and offer our support. In doing so, we can grow as individuals and as a community.

After reading More the Same than Different, I hope you learn as much from Lorraine about what it means to include, respect, and empower people as I have from knowing her. In the end, we are greater as a whole than the sum of our parts.

Erin Knox, PT, DPT
Physical Therapist
Tucson, AZ

# More The Same Than Different

What I Wish People Knew About Respecting and Including People with Disabilities

## Introduction

The shrill of the phone ringing in my dorm room during the predawn hours of that morning in late October 1987 only added to the chill in the air. I knew that whoever was calling at that time of day did not have good news, and the flatness of my mother's voice confirmed it.

"Your brother has been in a car accident," she said grimly. "The extent of his injuries is unclear right now, but doctors think he damaged his spinal cord. He is not moving his legs on his own. Dad and I are flying out to where he is in a few hours, and we will let you know more information as soon as we have it."

The thoughts swirling around in my head made me hang up the phone in a daze. It seemed like all the sadness I had ever felt in my life made its way to the pit of my belly and sunk as it combined with the weight of the overwhelming confusion. My brother, paralyzed? It couldn't be true. This could happen in other families, but not to us. Since I had been born with cerebral palsy, our family already knew what it was like to have a member who used a wheelchair, so didn't that make us exempt? What would be the point otherwise?

My thoughts spiraled downward as the morning wore on. Since he is only seventeen months older than I am, I don't think he was old enough to understand that when my parents spent time with me in therapy as a young child, the time spent away from him wasn't personal. As we got older, he always emptied the dishwasher and fed the dog because I wasn't capable of doing so. Resentment ran deeper when he got his learner's permit. Since I couldn't drive, he took me to appointments and sports practices, and along the way, he often took his feelings out on me as well.

"I have to do everything for you," he would yell. "It's just not fair!"

"Sometimes I wish you could live my life for just one day," I would counter. "You have no idea what it is like to live with a disability!"

So, as I sat in my room that morning waiting for news, I had to wonder if the universe had granted my wish just to spite me.

"I didn't really mean it!" I screeched, from the deepest place in my soul. But nobody heard me.

If I were being totally honest about my feelings that day, in the midst of my grief, I was a little lost and resentful myself. If my brother was going to be a wheelchair user, what did that mean for me? Would I lose my place in my family? Would his need for more attention mean that my parents and older sister would love me less? Was that the way he felt throughout our childhood? The heaviness of the guilt threatened to crush me. And it might have done so if my worry for my brother hadn't been so intense. How could I possibly be thinking of myself at a time like this? My brother was the one who needed help at the time, and that overshadowed everything I was feeling about myself.

His paralysis turned out to be permanent. In the months that followed, he went through rehabilitation and eventually resumed his life, albeit in a far different way than he had before. As I processed everything that had happened, I kept coming back to one question.

How could I help him?

I knew from experience I could help my brother with the logistics of living in a wheelchair, like learning how to navigate cracks in the sidewalk while pushing his chair and what the best course of action is when your wheelchair gets stuck in snow, but I wanted to go deeper. How could I help him? And could I help other people with disabilities as well? As I continued to ponder these thoughts and questions over the next semester or so, one thought stuck in my head. My brother, myself, and anyone else with a disability could adjust and deal with their circumstances most easily, it seemed to me, if the disability was not a factor to the people around them.

It has become my life's work to use my knowledge and communication skills to encourage, educate, and empower people to respectfully break down barriers between those with disabilities and those without disabilities.

My brother now lives in the Northwest. His wife, four kids, and his consulting business keep him incredibly busy. Although time doesn't permit it these days, he used to play wheelchair tennis and participate in wheelchair races. He hasn't ever let anything slow him down.

The biggest thing his accident taught me is that disability has an open enrollment policy. Anybody is a diving accident or a slip on the ice away from their lives being changed forever. Disabling conditions also tend to get more prevalent as people go through the aging process. Therefore, the issues that are so important to me in terms of respecting and including people with disabilities could potentially impact everyone.

Even if you are not affected by disability directly, you might still see its effects around you. Maybe a family member, friend, or coworker has had a stroke, developed a chronic illness or been in an accident. Or maybe you just want to know more. Whatever the reason for reading this book, I hope to share some tools and skills that will help you on your journey.

In all the writing and speaking that I do, the most common feedback I get is from people who say, "I want to be respectful of people with disabilities; I just don't know what to do. And because I don't want to be offensive, I end up not doing anything."

Sound familiar? If so, no worries. This book, as the subtitle states, is what I wish people knew about respecting and including people with disabilities. By the time you get to the end, my hope is that you have a better understanding of disability empowerment and some real-world ideas about how to help create that sense of empowerment along with the people with disabilities in your life.

### Disclaimer

Before we get in too deep, it's important for me to say that everything I have written here is not based on the "social model of disability" or anything nearly that definitive. Instead, I have shared what is strictly my opinion, based on my years of experience as a woman with various disabilities.

I have been told that people with disabilities comprise the largest minority group in the country (56.7 million people in America or 19 percent of the population, per the latest U.S. census). That means there are probably just about as many opinions on disability issues as there are people with disabilities. Other people with disabilities might strongly disagree with things I believe or that work for me, and that's fine. People who have different opinions make the world a very interesting place. My purpose is only to share my experiences, opinions, and ideas, not at all to tell anyone else that they are right or wrong.

I don't feel at all comfortable discussing disabilities that I am not personally familiar with. I don't like when other people try to speak for me, so I don't want to do the same for others, whether we have the same disability or not. I will therefore, simply cover my experiences as an advocate, a wheelchair user, and someone with a mental illness, and only touch on some other disabilities that I have personally been around. Having said that, there are some underlying premises that I believe apply to all people, including those of us with disabilities. For example, all people deserve to have their voice heard and to be treated with dignity. All people deserve respect and to be treated with kindness. Those things are universal.

I use my voice mostly through writing on my blog, a link to it can be found at lorrainecannistra.com. Throughout this book, I will emphasize some of the points that I am making through some blog posts I have written previously.

**Disability Awareness vs. Disability Empowerment**

To me, there is a drastic difference between *disability awareness* and *disability empowerment.*

My definition of *disability awareness* is that people are aware that individuals with disabilities exist in our society. It means there is general knowledge that there are many ramps in front of buildings because people who use wheelchairs cannot navigate steps. Or that some people who are deaf use a sign language interpreter to communicate.

*Disability empowerment*, as I define it, means people have that awareness, and they also see people with disabilities as equals; then they do all they can to help people with disabilities feel included and respected. An example would be if a friend wanted to invite me to his house for an afternoon, and asked me a few days in advance for the measurements of my wheelchair so that he could know beforehand which entrance to his house would be easiest for me to use.

That kind of thing is incredibly empowering to me.

In the above example, this friend would be accommodating my disability. Once that happened, I would hope that we would spend the afternoon sharing a common interest, because we are more the same than different.

# Chapter 1

## More the Same...

A few years ago, I was in Walmart and saw some twins who were about three years old. They wore dresses with the same pattern and the same style of shoes. Both had their hair in pigtails. At first glance, everything about them was identical. They were with their parents, and one little girl was riding in the front of the grocery cart while her sister walked along beside her.

I didn't think much of it until their dad approached me. "Do you mind if I ask you some questions?" he asked politely. When I assured him it was okay, he said, "This is my daughter Laura," pointing to the little girl in the cart. "She has spina bifida, and we are getting ready to order her first wheelchair. Can you give us some tips?"

We talked for about ten minutes. I explained that different features in a wheelchair would be important if they planned to push Laura in the wheelchair or if she was going to propel herself. Then we talked about seat cushions and the style of wheels and many other features that could potentially be important for her comfort. I was happy to help.

Later that day, as I was thinking about the conversation, it occurred to me that I would not have known that Laura didn't walk unless her dad had pointed it out to me. All that I saw was that she was like her sister. Lots of kids that age ride in grocery carts, even those without disabilities.

In her poem, "Human Families," Maya Angelou says: "We are more alike, my friends, than we are unalike."

I experienced this on a trip more than thirty years ago—the lesson so profound, in many ways it feels like it was just last week. I was in high school, living in Houston, and the sports team I was on for people with cerebral palsy traveled to a regional competition in Fort Worth every year. That weekend was the first time I had traveled as part of the team, and except for a few weeks every year at a summer camp for kids with disabilities, I had rarely traveled without my family.

Excitement brewed within me as I got in one of the vans to make the six-hour trip. Missing a day of school was simply the cherry on top of the sundae. I had worked out hard for the previous few months, training for countless hours in several events, and I was hoping I would do well enough to qualify for the national cerebral palsy games later that summer.

As soon as we hit the road, everyone began to relax a bit. Since I was in the passenger's seat up front, almost immediately I heard, "Hey Lorraine, turn up the radio. I love this song!" We all began to sing along with the music ('80s tunes are still my favorite), and as the miles passed, jackets came off, snacks came out, and several lively conversations were taking place simultaneously.

I was rooming with two of the other female athletes at the motel. They were ambulatory, and both were only affected by cerebral palsy on one side of their body. Therefore, they both walked slowly, with a pronounced limp, and they each had trouble using one of their arms. One of the girls wanted to call her parents to tell them we had arrived safely. I assisted her in dialing the phone number. Then she went to take a shower, and she was in the bathroom for a very long time.

The next morning the team had breakfast together. The coaches suggested we all order the breakfast special: eggs any way you want them, hash browns, bacon or sausage, and toast. Most of us were good with that. One of the athletes was not. The only thing that sounded appetizing to him was some buttered toast. He never ate much in the morning.

Both days of competition were filled with sports events. Track and field. Weightlifting. Bocce. Wheelchair soccer. Since we all were affected by cerebral palsy, each athlete participated in various events that matched their interest and level of ability.

Whenever it was possible, we watched the events and cheered each other on.

After two days of intense competition, most of us were ready for a break. The dance on the second night served as a welcome interruption. Since it was a regional competition, I met people there from other parts of my state and several other states. One of the things that made the dance fun was that we all danced to the best of our ability and did so with gusto. Nobody criticized what we couldn't do. There was one person with us, however, who did not attend the dance that night. He had pushed himself so hard in the previous two days that he stayed in his motel room with ice packs all over his body.

On the drive home the next day, a powerful thought occurred to me. Yes, we all had cerebral palsy, and that meant there were some things we couldn't do in the same manner as other people might. However, disability or not, we all have some commonalities.

- Who doesn't know a girl (or maybe several) who takes too long in the bathroom?

- Who doesn't know someone who likes to sing along with '80's music?

- Who doesn't know someone who pushes themselves so hard physically that it gets to the point that they must take a day or two to recover?

- Who doesn't know someone who dances in ways that some would consider unconventional?

- Who doesn't know someone who doesn't eat much early in the morning, preferring to wait until later in the day to eat a heavier meal?

Being part of that sports team in high school is one of the experiences that taught me to focus more on my abilities than anything else. And in doing that, I have discovered that in all the ways that matter, we are more the same than different. I do many things that people without disabilities also do.

Maya Angelou and I are certainly on the same page.

**There are some things that apply to most people.**
- We all get hungry.

- We all need water.

- We all breathe.

- We all have hearts that beat.

- We all have primitive reflexes.

- We all react to stress.

- We all rely on other people.

- We all laugh.

- We all cry.

- We all have a need to belong.

Does everyone have a disability, or does nobody have a disability? Is it a true disability when it can be corrected, like the need to wear glasses to see well? I don't know the answers to those questions. But I do believe that we all want to fit in somehow. Maybe when we approach disability from a position of power and see it as a difference instead of a weakness, then the playing field can be leveled and everyone can feel like they are on equal footing. Speaking from personal experience, feeling like an equal makes it much easier for me to interact with others and be a part of the situation in the moment.

When people treat me like I am "less than," I usually end up feeling like Tiny Tim (the little boy with the disability who everyone seemed to feel sorry for in *A Christmas Carol*, by Charles Dickens). That isn't a good mindset for me to be in, not even for a little while.

While it is true I live with some disabilities, that doesn't mean anything about me is broken.

# Chapter 2

### I Am Not Broken; I Don't Need Fixing

I don't like people feeling sorry for me.

At six years old, I saw myself as pretty typical. However much of the world saw me as "Tiny Tim."

I was a scrawny kid with skinny arms and legs, pig-tails in my hair, and a smile that was begging for a visit from the tooth fairy. Because of the cerebral palsy that had affected me since birth, I walked with crutches and wore leg braces, which weighed me down more than just physically. They were a tangible reminder that I was different from my peers. Wearing them made me feel as awkward as my unsteady gait.

I thought it was special when I was selected to be a poster child for United Cerebral Palsy representing the county where I lived in New Jersey in 1974. At a time when I was often excluded from games of tag and climbing trees with friends, I saw this opportunity as a benefit of my disability. I was singled out, but for once in a way that I thought was positive. In my six-year-old mind, this was important stuff.

The day came for the first photo shoot. My new dress, freshly styled hair, and big, brown eyes all reflected the excitement bubbling inside. Standing on the designated mark, leaning on my canes, I smiled big into the camera as the photographer set up the shot in such a way that nobody could miss my braces.

They took my picture.

The meaning was lost on me at the time, but that image was put on donation cans all over town that year in grocery stores, banks, and restaurants. The idea was that people should donate their spare change to raise money for cerebral palsy, and, to some extent, people should also feel sorry for me. Even at my young age, I took note of the stares, and the vibe from some people that my circumstances somehow made my life unbearable.

I am not sure I can adequately describe what it is like to be the object of someone's pity. The look in their eyes is a mixture of sorrow and "I am glad I'm not you." I've lived with it all my life and see it routinely in my day-to-day activities. When I can't reach something on a shelf or struggle to open a heavy door, most people rush to help as they give me that look. Some are compassionate, some are insensitive, some simply don't have a clue. But that look always leaves me feeling like I have inadvertently swallowed some lemon juice. Blech!

I don't think the decision makers who wanted me to be the poster child at the time were evil people. I am simply not convinced that anyone took the time back then to think about what that experience would mean for me in both the short and the long terms. The message was that, because I had cerebral palsy, I somehow wasn't enough, and that society at large should feel bad about that.

That's a whole lot of negativity to put on a six-year-old.

I know the same decision makers at United Cerebral Palsy had a job to do at the time. They needed to raise money for the organization, and I understand that an effective way to accomplish that goal is to pull on the heart strings of the public. Pity has been known to be an effective means for raising funds.

My parents tell an interesting story about that experience. I wore long-legged braces at the time, and halfway through my year as poster child, my orthopedic doctor told my parents that I didn't need to wear the braces anymore because they had served their intended purpose. The people at UCP would not let me be photographed as poster child unless I was wearing those braces. Their reason? They said I didn't look pitiful enough without them.

In our society, people with disabilities are commonly seen as "less than," but it's just not true. In terms of disability, many people distinguish between "us" and "them." Disability simply means that some part of a person's body works a little differently than the body of someone in the general population. Some adaptations might have to be made accordingly. In my perfect world, everyone would share that perception.

I often tell people that a good guideline is to treat people with disabilities as if they don't have disabilities, and then do everything in your power to accommodate the disabilities they do have. This concept was beautifully put into practice when I spent a holiday with some of my friends a few years ago.

One Easter, some friends invited me to dinner. There were about fifteen people in the group gathering for the meal. Several of the guys joined forces and pulled my wheelchair up the front steps. And they made sure I felt totally safe in the process. After being inside for a few minutes, I got to look at the table. It was set beautifully and was long enough to accommodate everyone. I looked closer. At the end of the table, there was a place specifically for me. These friends knew that the numerous legs of the folding table could interfere with my getting close enough to eat, so they set a place for me at the end.

---

**What they did right:**
At a special meal, my friends easily accommodated my needs in a way that was no big deal. They didn't consider having me sit elsewhere, away from the group. They didn't talk about the effort it took to make the accommodation. Because they had known me for a while, they simply figured out a way for me to be included and said, "We set a place here for you, Lorraine." That experience was awesome.

---

Many years ago, I was spending the afternoon at the park. I was a college student at the time, and I was visiting my parents on a break from classes. Out of the corner of my eye, I saw a guy looking at me every so often. The experience wasn't scary for me, but I did notice that his expression was somber, and after a few seconds he would look elsewhere. After a few minutes of this, he came over to me, got out his wallet, and tried to give me some money. The negativity never left his eyes. Then he started to walk away.

My shock left me speechless for several seconds, but with my dad's help, I was able to give him his money back. The experience took over my thoughts for a long time that day and made me look at the situation from several angles. I had so many questions as I pondered the whole thing.

Why did he want to give me money? Did he think my life was pathetic? Did he wonder if he would be able to live with my circumstances? Did I remind him of a relative or an acquaintance that he knew that had a significant disability and had possibly suffered? Did he think that money would help me to forget my disability somehow? Did he think that my having his money might make me happier?

I probably won't ever know the answer to any of those questions. I just know that I was pretty shaken up that day because it came across to me like he was giving me money because he felt sorry for me. And pity always makes me feel just a little less than human.

---

**What could have happened differently:**
A man sees me at the park. For some reason, he seems to feel bad about my circumstances. After watching me for a while, he comes over and says, "You obviously enjoy life. That is nice for me to see. Have a great day!"

---

One response pities. The other empowers. See the difference?

Do you consider people with flat feet to have a disability? No? Why not? There are certainly some things people with flat feet can't do as well as someone who doesn't have flat feet. Sometimes people must make various adjustments in the shoes they wear or how much they walk without resting because they have flat feet. Do you consider someone who has flat feet to be "less than"? Would you think it was okay for someone to talk in a louder tone of voice or only talk to the person accompanying them because of the assumption that people with flat feet are just not competent?

If you answered "no" to any of the above questions, is it because you don't consider having flat feet to be a significant disability?

Who gets to decide what is significant?

And if you would not treat anyone who has flat feet differently because their disability is "no big deal," why would it be okay to treat anyone with any kind of disability differently? Where is the line?

I challenge you to imagine how you would feel if you were treated differently because of your quirks. Would the injustice make you angry? Would you do everything you could to show those people your strengths? Would you ask people not to make assumptions? Would you talk often about equality and inclusion?

If someone with flat feet isn't considered to have a disability in society, why doesn't the same logic apply to someone who has low vision, or who walks with a limp or who wears a hearing aid? We all have disabilities in one form or another. Or none of us do, depending on your perspective.

I understand that everyone in society is the sum of their experiences, and as such, many people perceive my disability to be a bad thing. I do not share that attitude toward my circumstances. My hope is that, as others spend more time with me, they will see my differences simply as part of what makes me unique.

The more I speak to people about disability issues, the more a certain question comes up. In fact, almost everyone I know asks it at some point. It goes something like this: "Hey, Lorraine, if you could take a pill that would take away your cerebral palsy completely, like it had never happened, would you take it?"

My answer is simple: "Probably not."

I am never going to deny that there are aspects of cerebral palsy that can be a nightmare sometimes.

There are some days where my pain and spasms are so bad that I feel like the Tin Man with an empty oil can. And not being able to drive has made me feel as helpless as an overturned turtle more often than I care to admit. I can never decide to go to a 7:30 movie at 7:15. Spontaneous things like that are not usually doable for me.

But as I think about all of that, I also realize that it is only because I have cerebral palsy that I have been able to do things I have done. I excelled at adapted sports while I was in high school and was chosen to represent the United States at the International Games for the Disabled in 1986. (Unfortunately, those games were canceled due to terrorism six weeks before we were supposed to leave for the competition in Belgium. That was one of the biggest disappointments of my life.) Even so, my life would not be what it has been without my disability, and I would not trade some of the things that I have experienced for anything.

Does that mean I never wonder what it would be like to climb a tree or walk barefoot through the woods? No. There are lots of experiences I can imagine would be exceptionally cool. I just do not think I would be willing to give up the life that I have lived in exchange for doing the things I can't do.

Although different people believe different things, my Christian faith has helped me to be content in my physical circumstances. Of all the big goals and dreams that I have for my life, none of them include walking independently. Lots of people with disabilities put lots of energy into regaining strength and function. More power to them. But since I have never known any different, that just isn't me. Instead, I exercise regularly only to maintain the abilities I have. Most of the time, my focus is elsewhere. I like to believe I am pretty positive about my circumstances and hope that people around me will be the same.

Most people who I have encountered have good intentions even when it doesn't come across that way.

Several years ago, I went on my first road trip in a long time. Starting out before sunrise, my caregiver and I stopped at a McDonald's for breakfast. Close to the entrance, a woman stepped out and held the door for us. I thanked her. I thought that would be the end of the interaction, but it wasn't.

"I know how hard your life is," she responded. "I was in a wheelchair for several months."

She meant well. I don't want to diminish that aspect of what happened at all. My impression was that she wanted to share her experience to show her support.

I get that. Really, I do.

But what she said came out differently. What she meant as solidarity came across as sadness. Her pity was obvious as she shared her story.

Did she think my life was bad—that everything that I went through because of my disability was negative? Just like the man at the park, she would be mistaken. And if I had that attitude, it would eat me alive.

I would be the first to admit that when my strength is stripped away, some days simply suck. But isn't that true for everyone? Why did she feel the need to set me apart? Just because some people perceive my circumstances as difficult shouldn't mean that it is socially acceptable to feel sorry for me. Most of my life is pretty great.

It would never occur to me to go up to a stranger in a public place and say something like, "I see you have acne. My cousin has acne. It must be so embarrassing for you."

Why wouldn't I ever do that? Because the experience of a stranger only has the potential to be like my own. I don't want to judge how someone else might respond to that circumstance because I am not them.

To make matters worse, a different woman made similar comments as she held the door open for us when we left. "I know your hardship," she said. "My mother has been in a wheel-chair since I was sixteen."

Both of the women chose to look at a single thing that I deal with and presume it carries a downbeat meaning that applies to the rest of my life. I mean, sometimes I don't like that I am short. That characteristic can be frustrating, like when people in a crowd stand up in front of my wheelchair. When that happens, I can't see anything going on. But the fact that I am short doesn't take away from the amazing life that I live.

If a stranger took the time to seek you out and express sympathy for your situation, even though you don't see it as a bad thing, wouldn't that put a damper on your day?

17

**What could have happened differently:**
Look me in the eye. Smile. Ask me my name. Wish me a good day. Leave it at that. Adding sweetness to my experience will lighten my load.

**What they did right:**
As a wheelchair user, I always appreciate people holding doors open for me. Navigating my wheelchair through a door while trying to balance enough to keep it open at the same time can be tricky, even when someone is with me. That kindness was helpful.

I have known my friend Amy for many years. She also happens to be a wheelchair user. She "runs" marathons and half marathons, mentors kids with disabilities, and is active in her church. I have heard her talk about her frustration when people treat her differently from the strong, capable, independent woman that she is.

I can totally relate.

The statement that Amy uses to sum up how the public can be helpful to people with disabilities is both beautiful and profound: "One of the main ways to help reduce the obstacles that people with disabilities face every day is simply not to be one."

A good guideline is to always treat people with disabilities with kindness, respect, and dignity. I'm pretty sure that is how anyone would want to be treated in the same situation.

One of the ways to treat people with disabilities respectfully is to use empowering language.

# Chapter 3

## The Importance of What You Say

### Sticks and Stones May Break My Bones...

I am not comfortable with the word *handicapped.* The word has been around for many years, and I know many people use it frequently. I believed for a long time that it was taken from the phrase "hand in cap," implying that the only thing people with disabilities can do effectively is beg. That is why I've considered the word to be so offensive. Recently I've learned that isn't true, although I do know several people who use the term when referring to people with disabilities. The word "handicapped" still rubs me the wrong way because I believe there are much more more positive ways to refer to people with disabilities.

I have heard that some people prefer the word *handicapped* to the word *disability* because to them the word *disability* means "not able" whereas the word *handicapped* simply means that something impedes or makes their progress slower. I can easily see that logic, and I wholeheartedly say, "to each his own." I know different phrases are always going to mean different things to different people.

### Accessible Parking

Whenever I talk about the use of the word *handicapped,* one of the questions that usually comes up is a valid one. "What do you call the parking?"

My preference is to call a designated parking spot *accessible* rather than *handicapped.*

**Person-First Language**

Being called a "person with a disability" is my preference. This is called person-first language. Someone referring to me as a "woman who uses a wheelchair" feels much more respectful than "the wheelchair girl." (Yes. I have had people call me that.) I will always say people are infinitely more than their disabilities. We are people first. This is another phrase that means different things to different people. The best bet is to ask people what their preference is and go with that.

**"Retarded"**

NEVER use the word *retarded*. I know it is the past tense of the verb *retard* which means "to slow." I have an aversion to the word when it is used to describe a certain group of people. That is just wrong on so many levels. It's so low. I cannot think of a single time that I have heard someone use that word in a positive context in recent years. As a rule, I encourage people to refrain from using a label for anyone with a disability that you would be offended by if someone used it to describe you. The more appropriate term is *intellectual disability*.

**Wheelchair user vs. wheelchair bound**

I use a wheelchair for mobility. It is my way of getting from point A to point B. My butt is not attached to the seat with Velcro. I get out of my wheelchair and into bed every night. My wheelchair is a tool. Therefore, I am a "wheelchair user." I also move in and out of my wheelchair several times each day: to get in bed, into the shower, to use my parallel bars, or to transfer in and out of a car. I am not always in my wheelchair. Therefore, I am not wheelchair bound.

**Power chair vs. Electric chair**

I use a power wheelchair not an "electric chair." The latter is reserved for criminals who have done very bad things. It should not refer to the mode of transportation used by some people with disabilities.

**I'm not a victim...**

I don't suffer. I am not afflicted. I am certainly not a victim or an invalid. The last word means "in-valid" and that is not the case for any human being. Instead, I like to say I am affected by cerebral palsy. My disability affects my life, the same way other things, like being the youngest in my family and living in the Midwest, have also affected my life.

**My cerebral palsy doesn't make me "special."**

I just don't care for the label. It was decided very early on that I would be mainstreamed throughout my education. I went to typical schools and learned alongside my peers without disabilities. My needs were accommodated as they arose. The same thing was true when I attended college and obtained a Master's degree. These days I don't call myself a "special needs" adult. I am an adult with the same needs as everyone else in society. To be accepted, included, and given dignity, respect, and choice. I need employment, a social life, a group of friends to connect with. The way I accomplish things may be a little different from what is typical, but I simply do what I need to do to live my life every day.

There are many things in my day-to-day life that are special to me. Snuggling with my service dog. A caregiver telling me they enjoy their job. Getting a phone call from a friend who I haven't talked to in a while. A handwritten note from someone dear to me, or a text that reminds me I am in someone's thoughts. When there is something to celebrate, sometimes I have a special dinner.

And I think I'm special, too.

I've heard people say I have a great laugh. That I'm a good writer. That I have lots of compassion.

A few years ago, I had a friend tell me that she had never met anyone who had such an interesting perspective of the world. I have had other people tell me that they learned a few lessons about how to handle adversity from watching how I live my life. Compliments like these are particularly special.

I care about the environment. Advocacy. Empowerment. Communicating well. I want to be heard. And taken seriously. I want my needs to matter.

I want to encourage other people, to have a positive impact, and to teach things that others might not already know. And if I change a negative perception or two in the process, then I have done what I set out to do.

All those things make me who I am.

There are all kinds of ways I believe I am special.

I just don't believe that my living with a disability is one of them.

**I consider myself to be able-bodied.**

I don't like to be compared to people who are "able-bodied." I happen to think I am extremely able-bodied because there are many things that my body can do. Often, I have been known to come up with creative ways to physically get things done, like stacking many items at once on my lap in the grocery store. Those things could not happen unless I was incredibly "able-bodied" in some respects. I just don't happen to stand or walk independently.

**I also think I am very "normal."**

It leaves a bad taste in my mouth to be compared to someone who is "normal." In my mind, there is nothing abnormal about me. Because of my disability, there are some things I do a little differently from most other people. And there are many other things that I do just like everyone else.

**Our conversation does not have to revolve around some aspect of my disability. It's okay to talk to me about other things.**

There are so many things that I can talk about. The weather. A great movie I saw last week. The guest Ellen had on her show yesterday. Your favorite food. How you will decorate your house for the holidays. A problem you are having at work. Where you plan to go for your next vacation... Get the idea?

I completely understand that when people first meet me, they want to find a common bond. And that makes sense because I think that is part of the human condition. May I offer a suggestion? Ask me what I do in my spare time before you ask questions about my disability. If our connection continues, you can always ask about my disability as you get to know me better.

Now, if a friend of mine wanted to have a conversation about a relative who was struggling with an aspect of disability and wanted my opinion, I would be completely open to sharing it. That is an entirely different scenario. What gets a little old is when strangers talk to me about that stuff because they seem to think that disability is the only thing I can relate to.

In the first chapter, I talked about a man approaching me in Walmart to ask questions about a wheelchair his daughter needed. I was happy to talk to him and share information I knew. It came across to me that he considered me a resource and saw me as being in a position of strength. He asked for my help.

What I object to is the strangers who approach me and talk only about my disability because they don't focus on any other aspect of who I am. When someone I've never met before tells me about their great uncle who recently had a stroke in the first part of our interaction, I want to be kind and compassionate. I also eventually want to talk about other things in the same conversation. In the past, when a stranger assumes that all I want to talk about is disability issues, I have sometimes wondered if they also think that all red heads want to talk about being red heads, or if everyone with freckles wants to talk about how a distant cousin of theirs has freckles as well.

It may seem like a small thing, but language is very powerful. The way a word or a phrase is used can have a significant impact on whether I feel empowered or patronized.

What you say is important. It also matters how you say what you say.

# Chapter 4

## The Importance of How You Say What You Say

**Please, talk to me in a normal tone of voice.**

Cerebral palsy only affects my ability to balance and means that there is a whole lot of spasm in my body. My coordination is off sometimes, and on those days, I need help accomplishing basic tasks. It in no way means that I am deaf or unintelligent.

When I was a seventeen-year-old recent high school graduate, I was ready to leave behind everything familiar and was looking forward to my future in terms of going to college with equal parts excitement and terror. But that wasn't going to happen for a few months yet.

It was early on a summer morning, and my parents had held a garage sale the weekend before. A few months earlier, my dad had gotten news that he was going to be transferred for his job, so we were about to move from a huge house in Houston to a small apartment in New York City. The purpose of the garage sale was to purge a bunch of stuff that would not be going with us.

One of the things that had been sold was a sofa, and the woman who bought it said that she would be back at the beginning of the week with some moving men to pick it up. On that summer morning, the phone rang, and my mother told the woman that this was a fine day to pick up the sofa. "One thing though," my mom said to the woman on the phone, "I have some errands to run at the time you plan on coming. My daughter will be here to let you in. She has cerebral palsy and walks with canes, so it might take her a few minutes to get to the door, but she will get there and can do anything that you need." A few minutes later, after briefing me about the situation, Mom was gone.

When the doorbell rang a few hours later, I had no clue that I was about to experience something I would remember for the rest of my life.

True to Mom's word, it took me a few minutes to get to the door, longer than it would have taken someone who didn't have a disability. When I opened the door, a very well-dressed woman stood before me. On either side of her were two men who could have easily been stand-ins for the Incredible Hulk.

The conversation follows:

Me: "Hi, it's nice to meet you. My name is Lorraine. The living room is this way."

Woman: (very loudly) "HI! WE. ARE HERE. TO PICK UP. THE SOOO-FA!"

Me: "Yeah. Mom told me you would be coming. It's in the living room."

They follow me. Then one of the moving men speaks up.

Moving guy: "That sofa is big, and I'm not sure it will fit out the front door, so we'll probably have to take it out the garage."

Me: "Okay, that's fine." I turn to leave the room so I can go hit the button that opens the garage door.

Woman: (turning me back around so I am directly in front of her.) "THE SOOOO-FA IS TOO BIG. TO TAKE OUT. THE FRONT DOOOOOR. WE. NEED TO. TAKE IT. OUT THE. GARAGE..."

Now, let's step back and get a little context here. I have had my cerebral palsy since birth. My family didn't treat me any differently because of it, and the neighbors and friends that I grew up with were used to my physical circumstances as well. I knew there were some people in society who were uncomfortable around those of us with disabilities, but at that point in my life I had not encountered many of them. I was also aware that the woman was only dealing with her discomfort; she did not have the intention of ruining my day. Lashing out at her wasn't going to help any of us learn anything. These thoughts were tripping over themselves in my head as I pondered the appropriate response.

But it turns out I didn't have to. Someone else did it for me.

Moving guy: "Ma'am, I think the issue is only in her legs."

Brilliant, Moving Guy. Just brilliant! I could not have said it better myself.

As I have moved on in my life, there have been countless times I wish I could have folded up that moving guy and put him in my back pocket. His sentiment applies to so many situations.

To the strangers who literally pat me on the head and tell me that it is good to see me out in public.

To the salespeople who ask, "Who is here with you?"

To the hostess at the restaurant who asked one of my care-givers, "Do you need a children's menu for her?"

Really. The issue is only in my legs.

---

**What could have happened differently:**

The woman who came to pick up the sofa introduces her-self in an appropriate tone of voice and talks to me without fanfare in the same way she would talk to anyone else. Ev-eryone involved speaks conversationally as we decide the best way to get the sofa out of the house. After it is loaded in their truck, they thank me for my time, and we all go about our day.

**What the moving guy did right:**

The moving guy figured out pretty quickly that I knew what was going on. As he observed the woman try to interact with me in a way that was inappropriate for the length of the conversation, he gently let her know that I could com-municate in a typical manner.

---

**Speak directly to me and never only to the people I am with.**

This is one of my biggest pet peeves. Unfortunately, it happens when I am out in public an average of about once a week. Mostly at doctor's offices and restaurants. It's like people don't want to acknowledge that I am present. And it can feel demeaning to me. It's one of those "less than human" things. Some days I can shake it off easily. And then there are the other days. After one particularly bad experience, I decided to write about how I felt.

*To the Staff in the Office Where I Had an Appointment Last Week:*

*I won't stand for it.*

*I saw the look in each of your eyes as soon as I entered the office. The look of fear mixed with pity mixed with "I don't know what to do." I said hello, and you all tried to avert your eyes, not quite sure how to respond. The minute you spotted my caregiver, I seemed to disappear. Maybe you thought I couldn't communicate on my own. Maybe you thought that my caregiver knew more about some of the details of my life than I do. You asked my caregiver for information about me—things like the status of my health and what issue had brought me into the office. You asked my caregiver if she had my insurance cards. You made me feel like I wasn't in your presence.*

*Let me tell you something. I understand. Really, I do. When I am around a group of people I am not familiar with, it can be awkward. And I get scared sometimes. The reason for my fear is that I never want to offend anyone or say the wrong thing, so sometimes it's easier and more convenient not to say anything. That is the safest course of action, and the only way to guarantee that I don't make any mistakes. I have been there.*

*But here is the deal. It also doesn't change anything. If I don't face my fears in situations like that, they will always be awkward and uncomfortable. And since I don't like those feelings, it makes sense to me to do whatever I need to in order to not to experience them.*

*I heard this quote once: "If you always do what you have always done, things will always be how they have always been." In situations like this, staying with the status quo is unacceptable. Because sometimes, doing nothing is the most offensive thing of all.*

*There is no way you could know how hard I worked to earn a Master's degree after I finished college. You didn't know me when I pulled "all nighters" to study for exams, and you don't know about the countless hours that I spent in the library doing research. I can't fault you for not knowing that I earned those degrees. But solely because I have a physical disability, you didn't think I could independently communicate the information you were asking for. You did not give me a chance to prove myself.*

*The caregiver who accompanied me to the appointment that day was there only because she provided transportation.*

*So I have a question, and I ask it as gently and with as much compassion as I have within me.*

*Would you have a policy in your office that said that you can only ask men for some information you need because you assume that women don't know the information you're asking, or you assume that women cannot speak for themselves?*

*Did you gasp? Because that would be outrageous, right? No business in the country would have a policy like that and get away with it. If that policy existed, that business would not be around for very long.*

*And yet that is the unspoken policy in your office and in many other businesses that have staff who think it's appropriate to look to my caregiver to communicate instead of to me. Although I totally understand that it was not intentional, and nobody got out of bed that morning with the purpose of irritating my day, assuming I can't communicate for myself comes across to me as patronizing and hurtful. It felt like none of the staff thought I was a person.*

*My cerebral palsy can make my life a drag sometimes. I cannot stand or walk independently. Therefore, I use a wheelchair for mobility. Cerebral palsy doesn't affect my mind or my ability to communicate, and that would be true even if it did affect my speech.*

*So I am requesting that the next time I come into your office for an appointment, be willing to stretch out of your comfort zone and give me the benefit of the doubt. Please treat my caregiver politely because he or she did an excellent job getting me there.*

*Then, return my greeting, look me in the eye, and ask your questions of me directly, expecting me to answer you with accurate information.*

*Because I shouldn't have to stand to be respected.*

*Sincerely,*

*Lorraine*

### Caregiver vs. Caretaker

A couple of days ago, I spent the evening in the emergency room. Let me just say that when a stone takes up residence in my kidney, and then invites several of its friends to the party, I typically don't have a good time. At least not until I get the good pain drugs.

A new caregiver of mine was keeping me company. In fact, the time we spent in the hospital that evening happened to be her first shift. (How is that for breaking in a "newbie"?) While I was there, I was in the middle of the usual hassles I have in hospitals. Nobody could find a good vein for the IV, and when they finally did, we had to wait several hours for the results of the blood tests. I was feeling quite proud of my level of patience until something happened that made my skin crawl.

After we had been there for an exceptionally long time, a doctor I had never seen before came into the room. She started asking all the questions I had been asked before, and then she told me I was being admitted.

I looked her in the eyes and clearly stated that I would rather go home. Then, without a word to me, she looked at my caregiver and asked, "Are you okay with that?"

My eyes scanned the room for a 2x4. The urge to smack something was suddenly overwhelming.

Just like almost every other adult in the world, I don't like being dismissed, and as an adult, it should be my decision whether I go home or I stay in the hospital. At least I should have been part of the conversation. This doctor did not give me that dignity. Instead, she chose to ignore my presence when talking about things involving my care. I decided in that moment that I had a choice. I could either let the situation be flooded with my anger, or I could try to understand where she might be coming from. I chose the latter.

After giving the matter some thought, a possible reason why she did what she did occurred to me. Some people consider those who are with me to be *caretakers* rather than *caregivers*. Let me explain what I mean.

I define a *caretaker* as someone who does things for someone else who doesn't know how to do it themselves. A mother takes care of a baby, for example, because the baby does not know how to meet his or her own needs. Doctors take care of their patients when those patients need their illnesses diagnosed and treated.

A *caregiver*, on the other hand, gives support to a person while getting input from that person as to what needs to be done. A chauffeur can be a caregiver. A secretary or a receptionist are certain kinds of caregiver as well.

I would be the first to admit that, because of my circumstances, there are many things that I cannot do on my own. I will also readily admit that without the support of my caregivers, I would totally be toast. No question. But if they were to do the things that I need to have done without my input, we could both get seriously hurt. They would also be taking all my power away. Feeling powerless irritates me faster than my dog comes running for peanut butter.

So for now, I will continue to work closely with my caregivers to accomplish everything I need to. I will advocate for myself whenever it is necessary to do so and give a little gentle "education" to people who otherwise seem unaware.

In my experience, sometimes doctors need "caretakers."

---

**What could have happened differently:**

After telling the doctor clearly that I would rather go home, she keeps her eyes on me the whole time and asks, "Will you get the care that you need at home?" I answer affirmatively, and she says, "Okay, in that case, I will go and get the discharge paperwork together." Then she leaves the room because she has gotten all the information that she needs directly from me.

The bottom line is that people with disabilities are a very diverse group, and I don't want to speak for everyone, but if you ever wonder whether to interact with the person with a disability about their care or the people they employ, communication should always begin with the person with the disability. He or she will let you know if, for some reason, they would prefer for you to speak with their companion or caregiver. The person with the disability should always be the one to make that choice.

**Take the time to listen**

After I graduated high school in Houston, I moved to Kansas where I attended Emporia State University. Coming from a huge high school in Houston, I wanted to go to a small school that was very accessible. Emporia State fit the bill nicely. In 1987 when I began attending, there were only about 4,500 students enrolled.

At the time (prior to the Americans with Disabilities Act being passed in 1990), college campuses were not required to be accessible. Because of the compactness of the campus, the administration of Emporia State had made it a priority to be accessible to students with disabilities for many years. I earned a B.S. in English with a minor in creative writing and went on to complete a Master's in Rehabilitation Counseling in 1994. From Emporia, I moved to Lawrence, Kansas, where I got my first job at a center for independent living.

My job was to help people with disabilities learn skills that they thought would help them be more independent. Sometimes my consumers came to me, and we worked together at the center. Mostly I worked with them in their homes. That was the case when I worked with a woman named "Mary" who was affected by severe cerebral palsy. She used a power chair, her body was small, and she had a significant speech impediment. When I met with her weekly in her apartment, she would often ask for my help getting services and appointments.

We would always start out the same way. I would dial the phone for her (she didn't have the finger dexterity to do so herself). Then I would hold the phone up to her ear. She would start by talking to a receptionist. If they knew her, it usually went well. If they were concentrating on the conversation and gave her all the time that she required to get across what she wanted to say, she could calmly convey what it was that she needed.

If she was talking to somebody new, on the other hand, things could quickly go downhill for Mary. They didn't usually understand what she was trying to communicate, and they wouldn't take the extra few minutes necessary to figure it out. Consequently, they would guess what she was trying to tell them and typically, they would just go with that, even if they were wrong. As this process was taking place, I would watch Mary's face fall and could only imagine how the sadness and powerlessness of being misunderstood so often could be overwhelming. Every so often the angry tears of frustration were too much for her to keep in. She went from empowered and hopeful to discouraged and defeated. The whole scenario was heartbreaking and hard for me to watch.

**When talking to someone with a speech impediment, listen closely to what they are saying. Repeat the parts you do understand and ask politely for what you don't understand to be repeated. Never assume what someone is trying to say. Take the time to let them tell you.**

As a last resort, Mary would hand the phone to me and request that I finish the conversation on her behalf. When I did that, the relief that I heard in the voice on the other end of the phone made me want to cry as well.

---

**What could have happened differently:**

The receptionist taking Mary's call waits patiently for her to explain what she needs. Because of Mary's significant speech impediment, sometimes the receptionist asks Mary to stop while she repeats what she thinks Mary just said. If she is right, they continue. If the receptionist is wrong, she goes back to the last part of the conversation she understands, and they go from there.

---

Taking the time to listen to someone with a speech impediment and receive their message adequately is one example of appropriate disability etiquette.

# Chapter 5

## Disability Etiquette

Sometimes people impose help on me when I didn't ask for it. And while I know they have good intentions by doing so, that can be incredibly frustrating.

**Don't make assumptions about what I need.**

While the sun was melting away the icy traces of winter and daring the world to adjust to the coming of spring, the adjustments that I was making in my life had nothing to do with the weather. It was late February 1987, and I had just started my first semester at Emporia State University a few weeks earlier. The prior few months had been difficult for me. Most of my friends from high school had started college in the fall after graduation but I had unexpected surgery and a long, grueling recovery. By the time I arrived on campus, I was healthier than in previous months but significantly weaker than I had been in many years.

The campus of the university is compact, making it ideal for wheelchair users, but it also has several significant hills. At the top of one such incline was the building that housed most of my English classes. Since that was my major, I had to go to that building often. I struggled to get to the top almost every day, grunting and groaning like a linebacker about to make a tackle, but because the hill was steep, I never quite made it under my own power. It was always necessary for me to ask for help to get where I was going.

After a while, the hill became symbolic for me. I had it in my head that if I could climb that hill independently, I would be successful in my college career. Not logical, I know, but intensely personal nonetheless.

One day I decided it was crunch time. I sat at the bottom of the hill, willing myself to get to the top and psyching myself up for the process.

*You can do this on your own. Go!* I started out. The hill between my dorm and Plumb Hall felt like Mt. Everest to me. I put my head down and my hands back, convinced that if I kept pushing forward, I would make progress.

*Keep pushing. Don't stop.*

It became my mantra.

*Breathe*, I told myself. *Don't stop.*

Suddenly, about halfway up, a guy came from behind me and started pushing me up the hill without a word. My heart sank. Just like that, I was defeated, and I had nothing to do with that decision. I had to swallow the bitter taste in my mouth along with the harsh words that would have expressed the frustration I was feeling.

I know the guy who pushed me up the hill was trying to do a good thing. His heart was in the right place. I don't deny that. But he didn't ask me what I wanted, and in the process, he took away what I was trying to accomplish. Therefore, he just wasn't helping.

---

**What could have happened differently:**

A guy sees me trying to get to the top of a hill. He comes up beside me without touching my wheelchair. He asks if I need his help. After I explain what I am trying to do, he responds by saying, "good job, keep going." On that day, those words would have been incredibly helpful.

**What he did right:**

This man saw that I was struggling, and he wanted to help me. He did not simply walk on by.

---

What did I take away from the experience? I feel the most respected when people offer to help and then wait for my instructions about exactly what I need. Why? I alone am the expert on my disability. Even though my strength can vary from day to day, I know what I can do and what I can't. What I need might be vastly different from what an outside observer may see.

I completely understand that it is human nature to want to help someone who seems to be struggling. But overcoming the struggle can make a good day great for me, and when I finish something that I couldn't do before, nobody can ever take that feeling of accomplishment away.

I need the power to make the choice as to whether I need help or not. When the answer is yes, I need to be able to explain to someone how they can be the most helpful to me on my terms. When that happens, we can all get what we want and everyone can feel positive about the whole situation.

There have been many hills in my life since my days at ESU, and I am confident that there will be many more in my future. Some will be easy to climb, and some will feel like Mt. Everest to me, but those challenges are mine alone to overcome.

That is, until I specifically ask for help.

A few weeks later I made it up the hill by myself. I felt the same satisfaction that I am sure Superman experienced every time he rescued Lois Lane. It was an amazing accomplishment.

I understand how hard it is to see others struggle. And most people, myself included, will do anything to ease that situation for both the other person and for themselves. In terms of my independence, if I don't struggle sometimes, I don't grow. And if people always jump in to help me every time they see me struggle, then my "I can't" list will never get smaller. I will never achieve something I couldn't do yesterday. Please don't take that away from me. Accomplishing little things (or big things) by myself is essential to my self-esteem.

So, the next time you see me struggle, before you do any-thing, ask if I need help. I cannot stress the importance of this process enough.

1. Ask a person with a disability if they need help.

2. Wait for their response.

3. Then, if they do want help, ask them specifically what they would like you to do, and follow their instructions exactly.

**Don't do it for me.**

Just because you might be able to do something quicker than I can, that does not necessarily mean that I want you to do it for me.

A few years ago, I was working with a new caregiver. We got along well, and I was excited to be working with him. At 29, he was a bit older than the caregivers I typically hire, and for me that was a breath of fresh air. Our similar beliefs lead to some great conversations, and I was enjoying getting to know him.

One day, I had spent the afternoon writing thank you cards to some people, and the supplies were still on my kitchen table when he arrived for his evening shift. While I was trying to clean up everything, I knocked a pen off the table. As I was moving my wheelchair to get it, my caregiver bent over and picked up the pen for me. And that was logical because it's common courtesy to pick something up for someone, but to me, in that moment, it seemed like he didn't think I had the ability to pick up the pen by myself. Reality is that I could not pick up the pen as easily as he would have. He certainly could have picked it up and put it on the table with much more speed and agility than me.

But on that day, I wanted to do it myself.

I wanted to see if I could bend my waist and maintain my balance enough to retrieve that pen myself, and if somebody always automatically picks up the pen for me, I will never know or expand what I can do on my own.

People automatically doing things for me doesn't always make my life easier.

---

**What could have happened differently:**
I knock a pen off the table with a caregiver nearby.

The caregiver says, "Would you like me to pick up the pen for you, or would you rather do it yourself?

"I would like to give it a try."

"Okay," he responds, "let me know if you need my help."

"Thanks. Will do."

**Don't stare.**

I bet most people believe that staring at people with disabilities is a thing of the past, right? "C'mon Lorraine. Nobody does that anymore. It's rude. It's disrespectful. People only stared at those with disabilities in the '50s. It wouldn't happen today. It just wouldn't."

Let me tell you something. The 1950s called. They want their behavior back.

I know most people are not trying to be unkind or give me the message that I am different. They don't have to say anything. The stare says it all.

"How do you manage?"

"Is your life depressing?"

"Oh, you poor thing."

"Is it too much to take?"

"I don't know if I can live the way you do…"

Sometimes it isn't about any of that. People simply wonder how I get things done. Sometimes I explain. And on some days…

It was a summer evening a few years back. The days were long and green outside and a new caregiver was still green behind the ears. He had just started the process of learning the ropes. The sun was setting, and we had just finished making dinner. As he plated the food, I invited him to eat with me, and after he accepted, we sat in silence at the start of the meal, not really familiar enough with each other to attempt much conversation.

After a few minutes, I could tell he was watching, not in a bad way, but he was taking note of the fact that I ate most of my meal before I stopped to take a sip of water.

He stared but remained quiet.

During his next shift, later that week, he was preparing dinner once again, and he randomly said, "For this meal, we are going to slow down and drink between bites instead of gobbling the food up so fast." He said it with the authority that told me he had decided it was up to him to correct my "bad table manners." I was caught off guard at first, and then gently told him he needed to take a step back.

If he had asked, I would have explained that my cerebral palsy limits my finger dexterity, which in turn can make it difficult to switch back and forth between holding utensils and grasping a cup. To make things easier on myself, sometimes I eat first.

A few months earlier I was with another caregiver. We had spent the morning shopping downtown when we decided we were hungry. Sitting in a crowded, noisy restaurant about an hour later, it came time to pay the bill. With both hands, I fumbled in my purse for a bit, and after several attempts, successfully clutched my credit card and put it on the table. His impatience was obvious.

He stared.

After a minute, he said, "It really would be easier if you carried cash in situations like this." He was not thinking about the fact that the limited finger dexterity I have makes holding a credit card much easier than counting out currency.

I had an appointment a few weeks back. The temperature had dropped while I was in the office, and the guy who held the door open for me casually asked me where my jacket was. I typically don't wear one and told him so.

He stared.

He didn't realize that bulky winter coats are extremely confining for me and make it much more difficult for me to push my wheelchair. The quickest way for me to get out of the cold is to zip my hoodie up to my chin and make sure my gloves stay dry.

One of my hobbies is wheelchair ballroom dance, and the reaction tends to be the same when I show people my dance videos. It doesn't make sense to most that I am dressed in a formal gown and take extra care to make sure that my hair and my makeup are perfect, all while wearing tennis shoes. They look confused, and some communicate their disapproval, telling me that the tennis shoes take away from my performance. They don't understand that I need the support of tennis shoes for balance, and if I wore any other shoes, particularly dress ones, chances are good that I would fall out of my wheelchair while I was dancing.

I completely understand that the day-to-day details of my disability are not something many others consider. When they only look at something that I do on the surface, it is easy for them to wonder why I don't accomplish some tasks in the same way that most other people would. Most of the time, I can shake that stuff off as well-meant ignorance and not let it get under my skin.

My objection only comes when people look at the way I do things without asking my motivation, and then quickly decide out of context that there is a better way.

These days whenever I have a new caregiver who is trying to learn my routine, I sincerely request that they ask questions instead of making assumptions. Things usually work out better that way for everyone.

My disability affects me in a million different ways that many people don't have to think about. When they make suggestions, I realize most of them have the best of intentions.

However, my reality is that I have lived with my disability all my life, and over time I have figured out how to do what I need to do in the way that works best for me. If someone truly wants to know why I do some things a certain way, I am happy to tell them. Really. But that doesn't mean that their questions are always appropriate, and it shouldn't mean that it is always necessary for me to defend my actions.

On days when I don't have enough emotional energy to explain what I am doing, I honestly feel I shouldn't have to.

As a wheelchair user, some days it's easier to just take the stares.

**Don't make assumptions about my faith.**

The fact that I have a disability does not mean that I don't have enough faith. (I get told that about every six months or so.)

My faith is a very important aspect of my life. Since it goes beyond the scope of this book, I will not go into much detail about it. I will say that on numerous occasions, strangers have told me that since I use a wheelchair, God must be punishing me for my lack of faith. For the record, I don't think that is true.

Other people sometimes have a different opinion. The last time two young men tried to heal me of my disability was on January 21, 2017. Since it hadn't happened in a very long time, the whole thing shook me to my core.

On that Saturday, I went to the Women's March in Topeka. Andrea, a close friend of mine asked me to accompany her— kind of a spur of the moment thing. Enthusiastically, I accepted.

I really wanted to go. It felt good to be surrounded by people (both women and men) from all walks of life who were concerned about the same issues I am.

It seemed the theme for the day was solidarity. That we would all stand together as one group and fight for justice, equality, and hope. We weren't alone in our struggles. Other people understood them. There were all kinds of speakers. And I even saw a few people that I knew. It was a good time.

Toward the end of the event, two young men came up and said hello. Then they started asking questions. What was my name? Why was I in a wheelchair? Is your disability progressive? (It isn't.) That is when they asked what they really wanted. Can we pray for you?

I'm not inclined to deny anyone that request. Prayer is a nice thing that usually comes from a good place in people. I was not expecting what happened next when I accepted.

These two men closed their eyes and laid their hands on me. They started praying that God would strengthen my bones and muscles and tendons so that I could rise and walk. I was stunned. I couldn't move. Couldn't speak. Could barely breathe. And it only got worse.

After they finished praying for me, one of the young men asked me if I felt any different. When I said I didn't, they prayed again. When it failed to work a second time, they walked away. I'm sure they thought their prayers didn't work because I didn't have enough faith.

Sometimes I wish I were a little faster on my feet. (No pun intended.) Several minutes after the encounter, I could come up with about eighty-seven things that would have been appropriate to say. But as they were standing there, disappointed that I wasn't walking, all word and thought eluded me.

It is hard to describe what I was feeling in that moment. Sadness. Disappointment. Utterly misunderstood. Did they think my life, as it is, was not worth living? Did they think their prayer was going to "save" me? There is no way to know exactly what they were thinking, but I think it is safe to say that none of their assumptions about my life were positive.

The thing that struck me was that they were not preaching the gospel. If that had been what they wanted to do, they could have spoken to anyone in that crowd. Instead, they singled me out. Of all the people at that gathering, they assumed I needed to be "healed." In this event that exuded solidarity, I was the only one they focused on.

My friend Andrea, standing next to me through all this, has known me for more than 20 years. After the two men left, she asked me if she could go tell them that we were offended by what they had done. I nodded. She took off after them. Her purpose was not to be unkind in any way; she simply wanted to let them know how their actions had come across to us.

I'm not one to often speak about my faith. Although it is vitally important to me, I don't like to push my beliefs on other people. I also don't like the experience of having them do the same to me. It makes me uncomfortable.

I believe in a God who can do anything. Therefore, if He wanted me to walk, I would be walking. And since I am not walking, God must want me to be in the situation I am in. And I am okay with that. I will continue to be okay with that until God decides to do something different.

I also believe that only things that are broken need to be healed. A strained relationship. Someone who is suffering. A weary soul. My lack of balance and coordination simply doesn't qualify. At least not in my opinion.

When I was in college, I was part of a weekly Bible study. That is where I was introduced to John chapter 9. This particular section of Scripture talks about a blind man who the disciples brought to Jesus.

They asked Him, "Who sinned Lord, this man or his parents, that he was born blind?"

Jesus answered them. "Neither one. This happened so that the work of God could be displayed in his life."

Ahhhh. I get it now.

I know many people who believe that the work of God that Jesus is referring to in this passage is His restoring sight to the blind man. I have studied this passage thoroughly both in group Bible studies and in conversations with my pastor. I believe the work of God is displayed in my life every time He gives me strength and courage when I am weary and comfort when I am scared. There are frustrations with my disability sometimes, but God always works within me to make it through another day.

I don't know why I was born with a disability. It's not something I spend a whole lot of time thinking about. I've always considered my cerebral palsy to be just one characteristic of the totality of who I am. This is how God made me, and He doesn't make mistakes. And if God can show who He is through my disability, who am I to wish my circumstances were different?

The young men who prayed for me on that Saturday thought they could make my life better by praying for me to walk. What they didn't understand is that I don't want to change anything. My life is great the way it is. And my walking at this point is not my goal. Not by a long shot.

Not even a prayer.

**Check your "ableism."**

What is *ableism*? Wikipedia defines ableism as "discrimination and social prejudice against people with disabilities. Ableism characterizes persons as defined by their disabilities and as inferior to the non-disabled."

This happens to me more often than I would like. The "handyman" guy comes to my house, and when I show him what I need him to do, he says, "We will need to check with your landlord first" because he assumed that I did not own my house.

---

**What could have happened differently:**

The "handyman" guy comes to my house, and when I show him what he needs to do, he asks me a simple, direct question: "Do you own your house or is this something we need to check with the landlord first?" He asks me questions in the same way that he would any other customer.

---

Or the technician in the doctor's office who was trying to figure out the cause for all the fluid in my belly. She looked at me and said, "Are you actually capable of having sex?" That is a direct quote. Would she have asked any of her other patients that question in that way? How would she feel if someone had asked that question of her? She could have just asked me the same question she probably routinely asks other patients. Simply, "Are you sexually active?" would have given her exactly the information that she was looking for.

One of the reasons I was so offended is because I believe it is inappropriate for a stranger to ask me about my sex life. Even so, it happens once every six months or so. Seriously.

I totally get that most people have an innate sense of curiosity, and they want answers to questions or information about things they don't know. That is human nature. The thing is, there are these things called boundaries, and they are supposed to apply to people with disabilities as well as everyone else.

I totally understand that the concept gets confused sometimes because there are times that people with disabilities simply cannot have the same kinds of boundaries in the same way as people who don't have disabilities. Case in point. Some days I am less than steady on my feet than other days, and therefore I need more help in and out of the shower. Sometimes the caregivers who I work with happen to be male. There are times I need them to help me in the shower before they know me well. I would not typically get totally undressed in front of someone who I just met, but my circumstances require me to do so. I can't say that I love that situation, but I have gotten used to it, and these days it just is what it is.

However, the fact that I cannot always have physical boundaries with people because of my disability should not mean that other people should not have emotional boundaries with me. If you don't know me extremely well, and you have some very personal questions about how I may do certain things, that is the one circumstance when I might suggest you do your own research. Google is ready and waiting. Unless someone is very close to me, and I choose to confide in them, the details of my private life need to remain private.

How comfortable would you feel if some stranger approached you in public and asked how you had sex? It has happened to me enough for me to come up with a standard answer: "You know what? I was wondering the same thing about you."

### Don't Take My Power Away from Me.

*If someone were to ask me if there was just one thing they could do to be the most respectful toward a person with a disability, my answer would be this. Give as much power as you possibly can.* There are many ways to do that. Ask questions instead of making assumptions. Offer as many choices as possible. Make it known to people with disabilities that their opinions and preferences matter. When making plans or decisions that affect me in any way, always keep me in the loop. In my world, feeling powerful is essential.

# Chapter 6

## Empowerment

I've said this before, but it bears repeating. I would be the first to admit that there are many day-to-day things that I simply cannot do. I cannot put on my own socks and shoes. I cannot do my own laundry, and there are times when I cannot get in and out of bed without assistance. Because there is so much that I need help with, many times things are not done the way that I would do them. And that is understandable. Caregivers have limited time with me and lots of other things they do with their lives, so sometimes things are done quickly rather than in the way that I would prefer.

Therefore, I like to have power in little ways throughout my day as much as I possibly can.

When I say that people with disabilities need power in their lives, and I apply that concept to myself, I don't at all mean to suggest that I want to be a dictator and expect people around me to follow my orders or cater to my every whim. That will never be the kind of person am.

Rather, I mean that the nature of my circumstances doesn't allow me to have the same choices in life other people my age typically do.

- When I want to go anywhere, I must work around the schedule of the person who is giving me a ride.

- If I want to use my parallel bars first thing in the morning, I need to wait until there is someone around who is willing to put my shoes on for me.

- If I want to chop veggies into small pieces on a day my limited hand dexterity decides to be disagreeable, I must make sure someone is around to help me.

Because I need so much help every day, I like to make all the decisions that I can for myself. Doing so goes a long way in helping me to feel less helpless and less vulnerable. Below are a few examples of how I accomplish that.

- My caregivers ask me what I want to wear each day for almost each article of clothing I put on.

- If they go to the grocery store for something specific, they call me when they get there to tell me the options and ask about brand, how many servings, and price. And that is imperative, because I want them to get me the same thing that I would get if I were at the grocery store myself.

- If we finish running errands, they typically ask me if I want to go anywhere else before we head home.

Along with many other things, disability can take away a whole lot of power and choice. If I am going to feel empowered, I need choices, and I need to retain as much personal power as I can.

**Ms. Wheelchair Kansas 2007**
In the early months of 2007, I got an application in the mail. A friend thought I might like to compete for the title of Ms. Wheelchair Kansas. At first, I laughed. I would describe myself in many ways, but beauty queen is definitely not the first thing that comes to mind. Somehow, I just couldn't picture myself in a crown and sash. But something made me stop on the way to the trash can to throw the application away.

As I read through it, I discovered that the Ms. Wheelchair Kansas pageant was not a beauty contest. Instead, women who were wheelchair mobile were judged on self-perception and advocacy skills and would spend a year traveling the state to talk to various groups about issues that affect people with disabilities. Since advocacy lives deep in my soul, I could get behind that. Besides, since the contestants were required to have a platform and give a speech about it, I thought it might be good practice if

I wanted to do more speaking in the future. I signed up having no expectations.

To my utter shock and amazement, I won. The honor of being crowned Ms. Wheelchair Kansas is an experience that I will cherish forever. Traveling the state and talking to various audiences was one of the most empowering things I have ever done. As much as crowns and sashes still aren't my thing, doing my part to promote disability awareness and empowerment is vitally important to me, and I was glad to do so in that role.

My platform for the year was "Use Your Power" because I wanted to encourage people with disabilities to advocate for what they needed and to never let other people take their power away from them.

One of my best experiences of that year was going to the Ms. Wheelchair America pageant in late July. And it started with a very positive experience when I was at the airport, on my way there.

Arriving at the airport with a caregiver, we went to talk to the ticket agent. Truth be told, I was expecting him to ignore me and try to get the information he was seeking from my caregiver. That is what usually happened to me at airports. This time, I was wrong. From the moment I said hello, he made eye contact with me. He asked me all his questions directly, including the best way for airline personnel to help me to the plane and into my seat. And when he wanted more details, he asked me more questions. He also never assumed that my caregiver was the only person who was going to help me. At the end of our conversation, he smiled big as he said, "Ms. Cannistra, have a wonderful flight." The whole interaction absolutely made my day.

**Here are some ways to empower me:**
**Let me keep my dignity.**

This applies mostly when I am in the hospital but also when others are doing some caregiving for me.

When I am in the hospital, all my personal power goes away. As explained before, I don't have much to begin with, but when I am in the hospital, I am completely at the mercy of other people. I must ask permission to go to the bathroom and wait until someone has time to help me. Other people also need to turn me in bed and such. It often makes me feel both helpless and vulnerable. That is why maintaining my dignity is so important. Some examples include:

1. Keep my body covered always. When it is not, make sure the curtain is pulled, or cover me with a sheet.

2. Tell me when a shot or some pain is coming.

3. If you can't find a vein and must stick me multiple times to get an IV started, apologize for causing me some pain, even if it wasn't technically your fault. The experience wasn't fun for me either.

4. Always tell me everything that you are going to do before you begin to touch my body.

5. Check in with me numerous times during a procedure or a process (like a bed bath) to make sure I am doing okay.

6. Ask me what I need and wait for me to fully respond before you do anything.

7. Ask me if I am comfortable.

8. Ask me the best way to go about providing my care. Do I have preferences?

9. Listen to what I say and take me seriously.

10. Make conversation while you are doing your job. That assures me that you are aware of my humanity.

**Make sure I am treated like a person, not a problem.**

A few years ago, two CNAs in the hospital were helping me with a shower. In front of me, they both complained about how long it was going to take since "I couldn't do anything for myself." When I got in the shower, they both quickly washed me incompletely and did so without a word. When I got out of the shower, one of them said to the other, "Okay, you dry her feet, and I'll dry her hair."

While I can appreciate that they were probably both overworked and frustrated, I cannot control that I need a whole lot of help, and the vibe that I got in that moment was that I was just a huge obstacle between a long day and the end of their shift. I remember thinking that I may as well have been a mannequin. The whole time I felt like I had been a bother.

> **What could have happened differently:**
> Before CNAs help me with a shower, they ask me all kinds of questions about the best way to go about the process. Once we have a plan in place, we start to follow it, and they tell me everything they are going to do before they do it. When I am in the shower, and they are doing everything the way we agreed on, they ask me questions about my life and what I like to do. They are pleasant and respectful the entire time. And I sincerely thank them for their kindness.

**Treat me like the adult that I am.**

These days I don't go to the hospital often, but recently, for the first time in almost two years, I was sidelined there with a bowel obstruction for about three days. I wasn't happy, to say the least, but several compassionate and kind-hearted nurses took good care of me. With one exception.

In the early morning, this nurse came to get my vital signs and check my heart rate. In the process, she discovered that my heartbeat was slow and irregular. She asked me no less than ten separate times if I had ever had cardiac issues before (like my negative answer was going to change at some point), and she panicked. She called the doctor, obviously incredibly distressed, right in front of me. When I started to tell her that she was freaking me out a bit, she condescendingly said, "I know it is scary to be in the hospital."

I have been hospitalized more times than I care to count. Being there is annoying and more than a little frustrating most of the time, but it doesn't scare me in the least. Her behavior on the other hand, was a different story. Her reaction to what was going on with my heartbeat was seriously making me scared. She defended panicking in front of me by telling me that "the patient has a right to know what is going on." While I agree with her on that point, I don't think any patient is going to benefit from any medical professional getting visibly distressed about what is going on with a patient's medical issues in the presence of the patient. In my experience, I do my best healing when I am calm and reassured.

**What could have happened differently:**
When my nurse finds my heartbeat to be irregular, she asks me one time if I have a history of, or currently have, any cardiac issues. When I say no, she excuses herself and calls the doctor out of my earshot. After they talk, she comes in to tell me what the plan is for dealing with my irregular heartbeat and asks me if I am okay with that and if I have any questions. Then we proceed accordingly.

During a visit to the emergency room a few years back, a nurse suggested I change into a hospital gown, and I let her know I would need help with that. A few minutes later, a nurse's aide came in and without introducing herself or a single word to me, began to undress me. I stopped her and introduced myself, and she seemed irritated by the interruption. In thinking about the interaction later, I had to wonder if she would have thought it was appropriate to undress another 46-year-old woman without a word if that woman did not have a permanent disability, and instead, had simply broken and arm or a leg.

**What could have happened differently:**
When a CNA helps me get into a hospital gown, she first introduces herself and asks my name. Then she asks me how she can best help me. Before she does anything, she closes the curtain to give me privacy and maintain my dignity. Then following my directions, the two of us work together to get me changed into a hospital gown.

Unfortunately, this type of behavior happens much more often than I would like. But there have also been many times when I have been in the hospital that Certified Nursing Assistants or nurses have gone above and beyond the call of duty.

Many years ago, I was hospitalized with a urinary tract infection and was incredibly ill. The infection had gotten a good grip on my system, and I was sweating profusely from a high fever, vomiting often, and in significant pain. Suffice it to say it was a very long, miserable night.

Since UTI's were a frequent occurrence for me back then, I knew the nurses on the floor I was on quite well. After she was finished with everything else she had to do, Stephanie, my favorite nurse, came into my room. She had several cool wash-cloths that she put on my forehead, and she positioned both me and my pillow so I was more comfortable. Then she sat in a chair by my bed for a few minutes and held my hand while I fell asleep.

It was a huge comfort to me to know she was there, and how much she cared about my well-being. Everything she did that night played a significant role in my healing because she made sure I knew that she was with me, and that meant more than she will ever know.

**What she did right:**
When my nurse saw that I was struggling because I was so sick, she was motivated by compassion. After she gave me medicine that I needed, she then focused on how she could make me comfortable, both physically and emotion-ally. She was constantly aware of my humanity. That made all the difference.

When I went to college, I did so far from where my parents lived. So after finals every semester, I would have to go to the airport and fly to their house for breaks. In my experience, stan-dard airline procedure for wheelchair users is that they are the first ones to board the plane and the last ones off.

One year the weather was particularly cold and snowy, which meant lots of delays in my travel. By the time my last flight landed, it had been an extremely long day. Because there was a delay in getting my wheelchair to my first flight, I missed the connecting one, and because of a storm, the last flight was de-layed by several hours.

Airline personnel have a job to do in terms of getting me on and off the plane safely, and while I respect that, sometimes I get the feeling that I am being treated like an issue instead of an individual. This particular flight was one of those times. I was exhausted. And every time I have to get in one of those aisle chairs to get on and off the plane I feel suspiciously like Hannibal Lecter. It's not pretty, and it has been known to irritate me like a bad rash.

Because I was the last passenger off the plane, and most of the other passengers and staff had left, the pilot offered to push my wheelchair to the baggage claim area, and I accepted. It was just not a time when I was up for much small talk, and I didn't have an abundance of patience.

When the pilot loudly and slowly asked, "Do you like flying on BIG planes?" my response was simply, "Only when they are not flown by ridiculous pilots." Yes, it was sarcasm at its finest. The long day had gotten the best of me.

---

**What could have happened differently:**
As the pilot pushes me through the airport, he asks me various age-appropriate questions. Where are you coming from? Is this city home? What are you studying in college? When we reach the baggage claim area, he makes sure I know the process of how to claim my bags at this airport and where to wait for my family, and then we wish each other a happy holiday season.

**What he did right:**
Taking me to the baggage claim area was a kind gesture that the pilot didn't have to do. He attempted to make conversation along the way.

---

**I don't like to "settle."**
No, I don't mean that I'm obnoxious. Because I don't drive, lots of times my caregivers run errands for me. If I give them a list, I want them to get me exactly what I asked for, not something that they consider to be "close enough." There have been a few times when I planned on making a recipe that calls for a specific ingredient, and a caregiver got me something they thought would be "just as good" instead of what I needed. I couldn't make the meal. That is frustrating.

If I ask for a specific over-the-counter pain medication from Walmart, it's because I know what I am asking for will work for me. Experience has taught me something similar will not.

This even applies to my preferences. I like to drink almond milk. Plain, original almond milk. Not vanilla. Not unsweetened. Just regular almond milk. I don't like the other kinds. When a caregiver has gone to the store, gotten another kind, and paid for it with my money or my food stamps, that is frustrating. If I don't like something, I probably won't consume it. At the very least I won't enjoy it.

What is most frustrating is when caregivers go and buy things for me and come back with something other than what I asked for simply because they weren't paying close attention. It is a different situation entirely when they have looked carefully for what I asked for, maybe even asked an employee, and the store does not currently have that item. In that case, I ask my caregivers to call me and ask me what I want to do.

Sometimes a caregiver will pleasantly surprise me by calling to ask me if I want them to pick up something at the store that I had mentioned needing a few days before, but had forgotten to put on a list. Or sometimes, when I ask a caregiver to run out to Sonic to get me a cheeseburger for lunch, they also get a "pup cup" of ice cream for my service dog when I didn't ask them to do so. Those kinds of gestures make for good days. I happen to love positive interactions like that.

# Chapter 7

## Positive Interactions

**When having a conversation with me as a wheelchair user that lasts more than a few minutes, get down to my eye level. Otherwise I feel like I am being "talked down" to.**

When I say that, I'm not talking about a greeting in passing, I'm referring to a real, detailed conversation. In that case, getting down to my eye level is going to make me feel more comfortable– more of an equal.

If someone doesn't do that, no matter how pleasant they are, it feels condescending. How would you feel having a discussion with someone who happened to be eleven feet tall? Would you be at your best during that conversation?

Pull up a chair. Look me in the eye. Be prepared for a potentially fabulous interaction!

**When hugging a wheelchair user, get on your knees if that is possible for you. I can reach you better that way.**

To some people this may seem somewhat silly, but I have found it is important to me. Although I love hugs, I don't happen to be the kind of person who gets them all the time. Not because I wouldn't love to, I just don't often have the opportunity. Therefore, hugs are meaningful to me for many reasons. When I hug someone, I want to put a whole lot of myself into it. I cannot do that if I am awkwardly reaching up to embrace a person. The simplest and most comfortable solution that I have found is to ask someone to get on their knees to hug me if they are able to do so. Once again, that is what makes me feel like an equal, and that way I can put more energy and emotion into the hug rather than expending any energy on the awkwardness.

One more word about touch and disability. Touch is everywhere in our society. Handshakes, high fives, or a tap on the shoulder are common occurrences for most people every day. That is not always the case for people with disabilities. Speaking for myself and some others I know, I can say that people with disabilities are most often physically touched for medical reasons such as making a transfer from bed to wheelchair or into a car. People with disabilities are rarely touched simply for the sake of touch. Most of us have been poked and prodded incessantly because of medical issues, and I can say personally, that all of that has made me crave informal personal touch even more.

There have been many studies in recent years about the power and importance of touch. Everybody needs touch, even if it is simply casual touch. So if you ask permission beforehand, and if you are comfortable, put your hand on the shoulder of a wheelchair user or squeeze the hand of a neighbor who just had a stroke. Sometimes that kind of connection can mean more than anything else you can do.

**Let your kids ask me questions.**

It's happened so many times. I am out somewhere in public where lots of people usually go. Target. Walmart. The grocery store. A restaurant. The library. A parent with little kids is close by. The movement of my wheelchair catches the eye of a little one. And they are curious. And everyone knows that when kids are curious, they are also full of questions. So they start asking. Loudly. And the parent is embarrassed. They quickly try to avert their eyes while they attempt to hush their child. And they walk away trying to pretend the whole thing never happened. It absolutely breaks my heart.

In that situation, I never know if the parent thinks their child is bothering me, or if he or she thinks I don't want to talk about my disability. Neither of those things could be further from the truth.

Please let your kids ask me questions about my disability. I would rather them know the truth then have them assume the wrong thing. I also don't want them to feel awkward around people with disabilities, and I fear sometimes when I see a parent hushing a child around me, that is what it will eventually lead to.

---

**What could have happened differently:**
A parent is close by with one or more kids while I'm out in public. The movement of my wheelchair catches the eye of a little one. They start to ask questions. Loudly. What is wrong with her? Why can't she walk? Does she hurt?

The parent is embarrassed and tries to hush them.

"Oh, it's okay. Please don't be embarrassed. I have questions about things I am not used to all the time. I am glad your kids are asking. My name is Lorraine. Is it okay if I answer whatever questions they have?" If I get an affirmative answer, then I have a conversation with the child(ren) who is usually delightful and turns out to be the highlight of my day. My hope is in the end, everyone involved is smiling, and the kids are one step closer to knowing that disability is okay and nothing to be afraid of.

---

If I can explain things kids are curious about, then there is more of a chance that they will grow up to be people who understand and are comfortable around me. And that is what I ultimately want from everyone.

There was one interaction I had with a child that will stay with me forever.

I remember in detail a day back when I was in high school. It may seem insignificant to some. I thought it was at the time myself. But the more years I have behind me, the more I realize that an interaction I had that day just might have been one of the most important of my life. That was the day I learned that heroes come in all shapes and sizes.

I was a senior in high school, spending the afternoon at the neighborhood library, doing some research for a report I had due in one of my classes. I walked with canes at the time and was standing at the card catalog (Did I just date myself? Grin!) looking up the call number for I book I needed. I was in the middle of the process when a little boy approached me. He must have been about five years old.

"Why do you walk so funny?"

I was used to the question. The curiosity of kids always makes me smile.

I gave him my standard answer. "Well, my legs are not as strong as yours are, so my canes help me to stand up and walk."

He was quiet for just a moment as if he was trying to soak in what I had just said. Then came his response.

"My legs are okay, but I cough a lot."

He looked confused as I laughed out loud and was even more puzzled when I asked him for a hug. After giving me one, he wandered away, probably never giving our exchange a second thought. For him, the whole conversation is likely buried deep in his mind, and like most other childhood experiences, forgotten as soon as a new one took its place.

That wasn't the case for me. Some people might wonder why a simple conversation with a small child had such a profound effect on me. It was because, in the space of one sentence, that little boy leveled the playing field between us. After hearing that I was "different," he was quick to point out a way that he was different as well.

There have been countless times in the years since when people have considered my physical difference to be a weakness. In some cases, because of our circumstances, some people have considered themselves to be "better" than I am. Sometimes that's hard. Sometimes it hurts. And sometimes life just isn't fair.

There have also been numerous times in my life when I have had to work very hard to prove to others that I am equal. And there have been those times when all my efforts are in vain. But occasionally, when I am having a tough day, I think back to that afternoon at the library, when a little boy reminded me that I was no more different than he was.

Can a five-year-old child be a hero?

I say absolutely!

I welcome kids asking me questions. If I can give them accurate information and help them learn not to fear difference or disability, then chances are good they will grow up to be adults that will be inclusive of people with disabilities when they encounter them. That is always a "win."

**It's okay to laugh and be light hearted about disability.**

I say that with a caveat. I happen to love joking about my disability because humor helps me to cope with the parts of life I find difficult. And I have found that laughter can usually soften life a bit. But that's me. Before you joke with someone about their disability, I would suggest that you check with them to make sure they would be comfortable with that. I define a joke as something someone else thinks is funny.

Back in 1988, I was a college sophomore, still a little naive about the way the world worked, and pretty solid in the conviction that the way I had always done things was the only way that made sense.

It was a Saturday morning in the spring, and because the rest of the week I attended early morning classes, I didn't feel guilty about sleeping in. Although on that day, I woke up a little later than I intended. After getting dressed and eating some breakfast, I remembered that I needed to go to the ATM to get some cash for some plans that I had later that night. If I am recalling correctly, some friends and I were supposed to go out to a movie.

"No problem," I told myself. I lived on campus at the time, and the student union was not too far away from my dorm. So I put my purse with my ATM card in it over my neck and shoulder so that I could still push my wheelchair with both hands and set out. I didn't think it was going to be a big deal.

I couldn't have been more wrong.

The sign was huge, so I saw it from several feet away. "OUT OF ORDER!" screamed the ATM.

Not. Part. Of. The. Plan.

Now, at this point, I realize that most other people would start thinking through their options. *Can I borrow money from a friend?* Or *"Maybe from now on I should keep a little cash in a hiding place in my room so that this situation doesn't happen again..."*

None of those things went through my mind at the time. To me, the only possible solution was for me to "wheel" myself to the bank downtown, about five blocks away. These were the days before debit cards were accepted in places of business. Visa was certainly not everywhere I wanted it to be. It was also back when I held the belief that I had to be independent at all cost.

My thinking told me that it was required that I take care of all the issues that I could on my own. End of story. And no, I didn't stop by my dorm room to get the gloves that I used when I pushed long distances or the strap that I used to keep my legs in place when they spasm. It didn't occur to me to do so. In my head, I just knew that I had to get to the bank before it closed. Looking back, I now understand that I probably could have easily found a girl who lived on the same floor of my dorm to give me a ride. I simply never considered that to be an option.

I set out. The trip was challenging, to say the least. There were several big hills that felt like they had a 70 or 80 degree incline. They ate my lunch. There were some cracks I encountered in the sidewalk that I would swear were part of the great divide. By the time I made it halfway, I was huffing and puffing so much I felt like the big bad wolf, except there were no houses in sight. "Keep going," I told myself, "you need cash for tonight."

So I continued. Eventually, the bank came into view. I breathed a huge sigh of relief. There was only one problem. By the time I arrived, the bank lobby had closed. I thought I was screwed. But then I regrouped. There was one option left. I was in a wheeled "vehicle" of sorts, right?

Swallowing both my pride and my nervous laughter, I made my way to the drive-through lane and carefully rolled over the thing that rang the bell for the bank teller. The speaker came to life. "Hello?" I heard. The voice was full of confusion. From the teller's perspective, I was too low to see. "May I help you?"

Even though I was tired, I couldn't resist the urge to have a bit of fun.

"Hey," I said, waving my dirty arms over my head. "I'm here to apply for a car loan."

There was a moment of silence. But then the ring of her laughter sounded incredibly good to my weary ears. After giving her the information that she needed, I asked for some cash out of my checking account. When I received it, she told me I had made her day. And she was still laughing as I turned to leave.

It's interesting, all the hills on the way home seemed to go downhill. And making that trip also taught me that a little humor can go a long way in turning a tough day around.

In the years since then I've gained both maturity and wisdom. These days, I know how to ask for help when it's necessary and to be okay with the fact that I need it.

By the way, the car loan never actually worked out. But I didn't really expect it to...

Thinking back to that day still makes me smile.

I love to laugh and be lighthearted about my disability. For me personally, it helps to brighten my day, and it tends to make the people around me more comfortable once they have known me for a while. This typically is very true in my working with caregivers.

Some additional examples of myself and others using humor about my disability include:

- Caregiver: "Lorraine, let me tie your shoe for you."

  Me: "Why? It's not like I am going to trip. Just sayin'."

- Caregiver: "What kind of taco shells do you want from the store?"

  Me: "The ones with the flat bottoms. I like tacos that can stand better than I can. I get the taco shells that fall over easily when I want what I call 'solidarity tacos.'"

- Caregiver (whose car broke down in the Target parking lot during his shift; his parents brought him another car): "I'm glad that worked out; otherwise we would have had to walk home."

  Me: "Yeah, that would have been a problem because, you know, I can't walk."

- One day when I was in graduate school, I had the unfortunate experience of being hit by a car. A neighbor in my apartment complex was trying to pull out of the parking lot. He was driving an SUV, and in my wheelchair, I was a bit too low for him to see. I got a concussion and a few stitches out of the deal, but the funny part was the nickname that stuck afterwards. Friends of mine started calling me "Speedbump."

- One of my favorite stories has to do with my pastor, Bill.

  It was a few years ago during a church service, and Bill was in the process of baptizing a little girl who was about two years old. The child looked out into the congregation and saw me, sitting with my service animal. "Dog," she cried out. "Dog! Dog!"

  Instantly, every eye was on me and my service dog, and I thought my embarrassment might turn me into a puddle of goo, and I would die on the spot. The sacredness of the moment had been broken. Hey, at least I was in church. No need to travel for the funeral, right?

  Bill, on the other hand, turned around when he heard the little girl speak. As soon as he saw what she was seeing, he said, "This little girl is praying. The dyslexia hasn't been diagnosed yet."

  The congregation roared with laughter as they turned their attention back to him. Bill had my back in that moment, and it was spectacular!

- One day, a former caregiver had spent most of his shift running errands for me. He went to numerous places and had limited time, so he did many things very quickly. Right before he left, I thanked him for working so hard and told him I sincerely appreciated all the effort he had put in that day. After that, I said, "Michael, you rock!"

  Without skipping a beat, he responded. "And you roll, Lorraine!"

  He laughed all the way to the driveway. I laughed for the rest of the day.

I sincerely enjoy it when my close friends and caregivers make jokes about my disability. Many times, through laughter, my caregivers show me they are comfortable in their job. Both my pastor and my friend Andrea have known me for almost half my life. Their being comfortable joking with me about my disability issues makes me understand in my soul that they accept every part of me. And that is a gift beyond measure.

I have found that using humor about my disability with the people around me lets them know that I don't consider my disability to be a bad thing. Conveying that message is important to me. In my world, humor works.

Do you remember my story about the Women's March? The highlight of that day was when Andrea dropped me off at my house later that evening. I thanked her for giving me a ride to the event. As she was hugging me, she said, "Don't give me too much credit, Lorraine. I only took you with me so that I could get better parking." Alone in my house, I chuckled for the next half hour. That was a good line.

On one end of the spectrum of respecting people with disabilities is practicing appropriate disability etiquette, which includes empowerment and results in positive interactions. The other end of the spectrum is when strangers call me "inspirational" for the wrong reasons or take part in "inspiration porn."

# Chapter 8

## Inspiration and the Concept of "Inspiration Porn"

Whether people consider me to be an inspiration has always been a sensitive subject for me. On one hand, I don't understand it because in my life, I simply try to play the hand I've been dealt with dignity. On the other hand, if I can live my life in a way that inspires some others, I am honored to do so. It's just that being inspirational has never been my intention.

A few months ago, I wrote a purpose statement for my life. It was an exercise suggested in the book *The Success Principles* by Jack Canfield. He is a man I greatly admire for many reasons. As one of the founders of the *Chicken Soup for the Soul* series, I feel a connection to him, having had nine stories published in those books so far. He has authored numerous books and holds the Guinness World Record for having the most books on the *New York Times* Best Seller List at the same time.

When I heard that, the "bestseller wannabe" in me was wickedly impressed.

So I was intrigued when I came across this book he wrote about success. In the first few pages, he talks about the importance of having a purpose statement. The theory is that if you want to be successful in life, you should know what your purpose is. And that way, you can make sure that all your efforts along the way to success are aligned with your specific purpose.

That concept made sense to me, so after thinking about my passions and what I want to achieve, I came up with the following personal purpose statement, which has been stated previously: "My purpose is to use my knowledge and communication skills to encourage, educate, and empower people to respectfully break down barriers between people with disabilities and those without disabilities." One of the ways I live out my purpose statement is to explain my understanding of "inspiration" vs. "inspiration porn." Both of these concepts can be barriers between people with disabilities and those without.

One night I shared a video to my Facebook page. In the video, Dr. Frances Ryan, a wheelchair user, says we need to stop calling people with disabilities "inspirational" because doing so portrays them as something other than human.

As a wheelchair user, I can understand what she means, and I happen to agree with her on that point, especially when someone unknown to the person with the disability gives the label. I said as much when I posted the video. The comments that followed led to a thought-provoking discussion.

What I found the most interesting was that my friends with disabilities were similarly put off by the word "inspiring," and there were a few of my friends without disabilities that didn't seem to understand why.

My favorite comment was from my friend Lindsey, who happens to have spina bifida: "My disdain for [this kind of] inspirational porn is that things that should be normal are inspirational when someone with a disability does it. I'm an inspiration for going to work. How is that different than my non-disabled counterpart going to work? To me, it implies I'm not expected to be able to work just because of my disability. So really, someone telling me 'you're an inspiration' is a passive-aggressive way of saying I don't think disabled people can be normal."

I don't like being called "inspirational" for doing the same thing people without disabilities do on a regular basis, like making myself a sandwich or working hard at my job.

There are some cases though when I am flattered when people call me inspirational. The difference is that I hope people are inspired by something that makes me uniquely me, instead of what might be an incorrect assumption about what my life is like.

For example, in the last several years, one of my passions has been wheelchair ballroom dance, and several times my partner, Brandon, and I had the opportunity to perform at various competitions. After one such performance, a woman in the audience approached me. She was in tears. She told me how much the performance had moved her and that she would remember it for a long time. Given how much work Brandon and I had put into making the performance as good as it could be, her positive words felt good to me.

An hour or so after my conversation with that woman, the guy who was filming all the performances asked me if he could put the video of one of our dance routines on his business web page. I agreed.

A few days later, I went to the page and looked for the video. It was there, and the caption read, "I thought I had problems..." and went on to say what an incredibly inspiring performance our routine was.

The caption he had written under the video gave me a very patronized and "patted on the head" feeling.

I know he had the best of intentions. He, unfortunately, missed the point. I dance because I think it is fun, and it is important to me that people with disabilities be portrayed in a position of power, not pity. He didn't see my dancing in the same way I did.

I emailed him and politely let him know that my life was pretty great. He took the comment down.

At the core of my being, I believe that everyone should be treated as equals. That is never going to happen if there are some people who are inspired just because I am employed or I have some hobbies.

Do I face more challenges than some people when I try to accomplish some things? Maybe. But everyone has challenges. I don't have to get kids off to school or daycare as part of my morning routine. I don't have a job at an office where I must be at a certain time. I almost never have to deal with rush-hour traffic. I simply do what I must do every day because the alternative, which would be sitting in a nursing home and staring at a wall while being cared for by strangers, would suck. For me, in order to live the life that I want, it is only about making the choice to do things that I consider to be productive.

And sometimes people watch me. Current or former caregivers or friends who know what goes into my routine have called me inspirational. And that is okay with me. Because they have a reason that is about me personally. They can back up what they are saying with some facts. So when I am called inspirational by those kinds of people in my world, I consider it a compliment.

One of the nicest comments I have ever received came from a caregiver who worked for me a few summers ago. He casually told me one morning that working for me reminded him to slow down. With a teasing grin, I asked him if that was because it took me so long to do things.

"No," he responded quickly, "that is not what I mean at all. I don't have the same challenges you do, and I can get up, get dressed, and get out the door within about five minutes of my alarm going off if I need to. That scenario is not possible for you because for you, getting dressed and ready for the day is a more complicated process. Sometimes, as I am putting your shoes on in the morning, you look out the window and make a comment about how nice the day looks outside. When I rush out of the house in the morning, I usually don't notice the weather. Working for you has taught me to slow down. That inspires me."

---

**What he did right:**
This particular caregiver took time to not only figure out my routine but to observe something that he considered positive in the process. Many people could perceive the fact that I have to do things more slowly as a negative thing and be negative with me because of it. However, this caregiver took notice of the way I do something specific and shared with me how that had been a positive thing in his life. It was a win-win because thinking about his comment made me feel good for days.

---

I had an online conversation with a friend of mine a few months back. She told me that when she found me on Facebook and took the time to look on my page, she was "simply amazed at all I had been able to do." This woman is someone I sincerely admire. She meant it as a compliment, and I know that, so I mean no disrespect to her whatsoever. As I read her comment, what kept running through my head were questions like:

What did she think I was doing?

Was I not supposed to go to college or earn a Master's degree?

Was I not supposed to pursue my hobbies or advocate for programs that would enhance my life?

And if not, why not?

Does the fact that I use a wheelchair for mobility mean that I should not pursue those things?

What exactly was I supposed to do instead?

If the people who say things like that to me are saying that they don't know if they could do what I am doing in the same circumstances, that is not something they could possibly identify. Nobody can give more than an educated guess about how they would handle a given situation until they are faced with it. If somebody would come up to me and say, "I am not sure, if I had the challenges in life that you do, that I could live my life in the same way that you live your life," as opposed to calling me inspirational, I would not be offended in the least. My hope is that if someone is inspired by watching what I do, that will motivate them to attempt to do something they never thought they could.

From where I sit, I simply live my life. Some days are fabulous, and some are messy. Sometimes I want a do-over about an hour after my day has started. And some days I wish I could rewind and live them repeatedly because they are so awesome. Life is just like that—for everyone.

And this is one of those scenarios where I hope people would treat me in the same way that they would want to be treated if they were ever in a similar situation. With nothing but respect, kindness, and plenty of dignity.

My preference is that people get to know me well before they put any labels on me, even ones that they consider to be positive. And leave room for the possibility that what you are intending as positive might not come across the same way to a person with a disability.

Make sure you have a specific reason for the label.

> **What could have happened differently:**
> After reading about things I am doing on Facebook, a friend sends me a message that says, "Hey, Lorraine, it looks like you are busy and doing things that you enjoy. Life seems to be treating you well. That's great! Let's catch up sometime."

In my opinion, it is fine to call someone with a disability "inspirational" if you are emotionally moved by something specific they do or something specific they have accomplished that is unique to them. Just because someone with a disability is living their life, that alone does not make them inspirational.

## Inspiration porn

What is *inspiration porn*? The late Australian activist Stella Young had osteogenesis imperfecta. In a *TED Talk* she appeared in, she talks about a member of her community wanting to nominate her for a prestigious achievement award when she was a teenager. Her parents had an epic response. They said the award was great, but their daughter had not done anything to earn such an honor. According to Ms. Young, "They were right. I had not done anything out of the ordinary if you took disability out of the equation." Ms. Young coined the term *inspiration porn* and defined it as "the misplaced admiration of people with disabilities because of their disabilities."

Last year, ABC launched a new show called *Speechless*. Now in its second season, the show is about a family with three kids. The oldest son, a character named J.J DiMeo, has cerebral palsy. Micah Fowler, the actor who plays the character is affected by cerebral palsy as well. One of the things I love about the show is that it explores the "nitty-gritty-this-is-the-real-stuff-disability-issues" that J.J. encounters in his everyday life, and he makes no secret of the fact that he hates inspiration porn.

J.J.'s younger brother Ray defines inspiration porn this way in one of the scenes of the show: "It's a portrayal of people with disabilities as one-dimensional saints who only exist to warm the hearts and open the minds of able-bodied people."

To me, that definition of inspiration porn nails the concept perfectly.

Some examples would include:

- A high school wrestler who purposely loses a match to his opponent with Down Syndrome so that the second wrestler can celebrate the only wrestling win he will ever have. The two boys are not close friends.

- The homecoming queen who gives her crown to another student with various disabilities that she has barely met.

- The woman I see at the mall who says, "It's so good to see you out in public."

- When my friend and I saw a little person at a hospital who was wearing a uniform as part of a cleaning crew, she said, "It's amazing that people like that can have jobs."

- Poster with a picture of a wheelchair user racing around the track that have a caption like "the only disability in life is a bad attitude." Stella Young once said that "a good attitude is not going to turn a flight of stairs into a ramp."

- Poster of an amputee with prosthetics climbing a mountain that says "What's your excuse?" There could be many "mountains" in front of people that have nothing to do with disability.

- When I was describing my experience at the Ms. Wheelchair America Pageant to an acquaintance and giving some details about the women that I had met, she looked at me in shock and said, "You mean some of the women were actually married to guys who didn't have disabilities?"

It's a bit hard for me to articulate why this concept bothers me. Any instance I see of inspiration porn is just another example of how society doesn't expect people with disabilities to live a typical life. Like my friend Lindsey said previously, it means that I'm not expected to be "normal."

Commonplace inspiration porn that I find offensive is when someone does something nice for someone with a disability, and it makes the news. Every spring there are several stories on the news and online of students asking peers with disabilities to the prom.

I think it is great for friends to spend social time together, and I am all for getting dressed up to do it. There is an excitement attached to getting a tux or a beautiful dress and putting on makeup—maybe even riding in a limo. All of that is good stuff, and it would be fabulous if every teenager who wanted to go the prom had the option to experience it.

What makes me cringe is when a student with a disability is asked to the prom by a student without a disability, and it makes the news. And typically, society eats it up and talks about how nice and "selfless" it all is.

For years I have heard stories about kids who were friends and went to prom together. Because they wanted to. It wasn't a headline. It wasn't a "feel good" story. Where does the concept of inclusion go during prom season?

I just get tired sometimes of the story at the end of a national news show being about a popular football player or a gorgeous cheerleader who could have gone to the prom with anyone, but instead they chose to go with their friend from elementary school who is on the autism spectrum or has Down Syndrome because "they knew it would make them happy." I don't want to diminish a gesture of kindness if a student with a disability would not otherwise attend their prom. I just don't like seeing news stories about it. I would rather have such gestures be commonplace because that speaks more of equality to me.

But inspiration porn isn't just reserved for prom season. It can happen at your neighborhood McDonald's...

Remember the guy with cerebral palsy who went into McDonald's and asked one of the employees to help him with his meal? It happened a few years ago. The employee closed a register and cut up the food, and a customer who was witnessing the scene took a picture. That photograph went viral almost overnight.

I will never deny that what the employee did was a nice gesture, and once again, it is not my intention to diminish his kindness in any way. Several people put some effort into finding out the name of the employee and relaying his actions to the store manager.

Did anyone bother to get the name of the man with the disability? In terms of the media coverage, it seemed like he was just used as a prop in this story that made so many other people feel good. Did anyone inquire if he needed assistance finding good caregivers or if he needed some other kind of help? Would anyone have been interested if, in that same McDonald's, a husband was feeding his wife who had an advanced case of multiple sclerosis? Did the camera get turned on when somebody held the door for somebody else while they were getting lunch at McDonald's? No? Why not?

People extend kindnesses to each other all over the world every day. Why does it usually only make the news when a person with a disability is involved? As far as all the news outlets and social media were concerned, that is where the story ended. Let me tell you the other part of the story that didn't happen to get covered by the media.

The former director of communications of United Cerebral Palsy in Washington D.C. wrote this story a few weeks after the event took place:

*The full story of the man pictured in a photo that went "viral" this week is even more touching than you might imagine. The snapshot posted to Facebook by a customer showed McDonald's employee Kenny helping Dan Garringer cut and eat his food. Many news outlets reported that Dan ordered his food, then requested some help from Kenny, who promptly closed his till at the busy Union Station restaurant and helped Dan eat his meal. More than one million people have liked and shared the photo on social media, with many commenting about Kenny's compassion and kindness. Kenny was given special recognition by the owner/operator of his McDonald's franchise.*

*What many of those commenters don't realize is that this photo speaks volumes to those who know the story of Dan's life. Dan has cerebral palsy and has striven his entire life to live as independently as possible as a participating and valued member of his community.*

*"People with disabilities are just like everyone else. We love life and being part of our community. We go to restaurants, stores, the movies and coffee shops and take Metra and public transportation to be able to experience life as everyone else does," Dan said.*

"*I know that Kenny is getting all of the credit, but, in my mind, he is representing all the employees at the Union Station McDonald's. They are wonderful, caring people who make me feel that I am just like everyone else, and they do not treat me like I am a person with a disability... they treat me like I am just Dan, someone that loves McDonald's fries.*"

*In 1993, Dan and his wife Clarina, who passed away last year, moved into a group home where UCP Seguin of Greater Chicago can provide the support and services he needs. UCP Seguin is an affiliate of United Cerebral Palsy, a nonprofit organization for people with disabilities.*

*Dan spent his childhood with his family but moved into a nursing home as an adult, where he met and married his wife. For years, he was told he was "too handicapped" to work. But after he connected with UCP Seguin, he worked with a case worker to pursue a writing career. For more than a decade, he wrote a column for his local newspaper, Suburban Life, called "The View from Here." Using just a thumb and forefinger on one hand, Dan wrote about human potential and advocated for people with disabilities to be fully included in life concepts neatly captured in this one image.*

"*Dan often wrote about experiences very much like this... and many times the opposite of this, as he was faced with discrimination, insults, and worse,*" *said Jim Haptonstahl, Executive Vice President of UCP Seguin.*

"*He has been overwhelmed by the reaction to this story. But he's good with it, if it promotes greater acceptance and inclusion of people with disabilities in society.*"

*United Cerebral Palsy and its affiliates, such as UCP Seguin, advocate for that greater acceptance and inclusion, providing the services needed to ensure that people like Dan have the care, education, employment, housing, and other opportunities they need.*

"*Every one of us has certain challenges,*" *said Jim. "Dan's challenges mean he sometimes needs a little help from his fellow community members. Kenny gets that. And that's cool.*"

*(DeButts, Shelly. "Story Behind Viral Photo Better Than You Think." United Cerebral Palsy: Life without Limits for People with Disabilities, 25 Sept. 2015, ucp.org/story-behind-viral-photo-better-than-you-think/.)*

The real story is about empowerment. It's about how much Dan Garringer can do independently, and how much effort he is willing to put forth to be out in his community. The media put an entirely different spin on the story and chose to focus only on a McDonald's employee providing some assistance to man with a disability. To them, that was news. But it was only part of the story. And that is classic example of inspiration porn.

---

**What could have happened differently:**

A woman is in McDonald's and sees an employee taking time to assist a customer with a disability. She is moved by what she sees and feels the need to know more, so she goes over to Mr. Garringer and asks him if he is willing to have a conversation with her while he eats his lunch. If his response is affirmative, she takes time to talk to both Mr. Garringer and the McDonald's employee. There is no picture involved because she wants to make sure everyone involved is treated with dignity and respect.

---

How cool it would have been if the focus of the story were about how the employees are open-minded and compassionate enough to help Dan feel included? That's the kind of story that I wish would go viral.

I long for a world where everyone is treated as equals, and people focus on the fact that I am a young woman before they see my wheelchair. And I know that even decades after the passage of the Americans with Disabilities Act, society is a long way from being where I wish it was. If stories about people being kind to people with disabilities continue to make national news, people with disabilities are never going to be treated as equals in this society.

Why does inspiration porn bother me so much? Because it magnifies the distance between people with disabilities and those without disabilities. It encourages a mentality of "us" and "them," and it makes me feel that, solely because I have a physical disability, society considers me to be less than. Nobody should feel that way. Ever. I have accomplished a whole lot of things in my life that I am proud of. And I am more than my wheelchair. I just wish more people would see that.

*Inspiration porn* gets in the way of empowering people with disabilities because most examples of inspiration porn portray the person with the disability as unequal.

The opposite of inspiration porn is inclusion.

# Chapter 9

## Inclusion

The inclusion of people with disabilities is what will narrow the gap between "us" and "them" and make all of society, both people with disabilities and those without, more completely "all of us."

It's becoming a habit every summer—one that I could get used to. Dale, my best friend from college, who is a teacher and a coach by trade, comes up to Lawrence for three days a week, several weeks in a row, and he works as my caregiver. The arrangement came about last year. I was short on caregivers, and he needed some employment in the summer months. It would be safe to say that the whole thing was his idea.

Given that we live several hours apart, he leaves from a small town outside of Wichita while it is still dark. He arrives at 8 a.m. and works through the day until about 11 p.m., and he crashes on my sofa in between. On the third day, he leaves at about 6 p.m., packing 40 hours of work into three days. Then he spends four days at home with his wife and family and does the same thing for the several weeks that follow.

The setup works well for both of us. It gives him the employment that he needs for the summer, and it helps me out when my caregivers are in short supply. That makes it a win-win situation. When Dale is here, he works like a maniac. He does a gazillion loads of laundry that he folds and puts away. He washes the dishes after every meal that he prepares. (He makes a mean stir-fry, I tell you. He even keeps the veggies crunchy.)

This year while he was here, we cleaned out and organized my shed; then he painted part of my carport, weeded around my bushes, and trimmed the shrubs in my backyard. He got up on a ladder and cleaned my gutters. We went through and donated some of my books and movies, sprayed my whole house for bugs, and took my service dog to the vet. He thought nothing of helping me in and out of the shower or helping me get dressed or ready for bed. Whenever I thanked him for his kindness, he quickly shrugged it off and reminded me that he considers me family.

Awwww. Right back at you, Dale!

Perhaps one of my favorite things that Dale and I do when we are together is to reminisce about memories we have from college. This year, one memory stood out above all the others.

It was probably during my junior year, and it had been an exceptionally long week. Dale and I typically hung out with a group of students from the Baptist Student Union. On that Friday night, several of our friends wanted to go bowling. I never want to be considered a party pooper, but spending the evening simply watching other people bowl (which was something I didn't think I could do) did not sound like my idea of a good time. I tried to bow out gracefully, telling everyone that I was tired and planned on spending a quiet evening at home reading a good book. It was the truth.

Dale knew me well. He said "Lorraine, if you come bowling with us, I promise you'll have fun. Please?"

Who can pass up a request like that from a guy who so many young women had a crush on?

At the bowling alley, several people did their best to try and get me to successfully hit some pins. I was given the lightest ball in the building. Many friends tried holding my wheelchair in various ways to give me leverage. One guy even picked me up out of my chair and put me on the floor, in front of the lane, and had me push off on the bowling ball between my knees. Nothing worked. No matter what we attempted, the result was nothing but gutter. I put my foot down when one of the staff offered to put those tubes filled with air in the gutters. I realize that he was trying to help, but even twenty-one-year-olds must maintain their dignity.

There were only a few frames left in the last game. Dale had been observing everything but had not said much the whole night. Finally, he came up to me with an amused look on his face.

"I know what the problem is, Lorraine." He declared. "It's the shoes. You don't have any bowling shoes."

With that, he took the shoes off his feet and replaced my tennis shoes with them. Then when it was my turn, he wheeled me up to the bowling lane and held my chair in place. "Concentrate, Quiche," he said. It was his nickname for me. He always had a theory that I had been named after food. Quiche Lorraine. Get it?

I took a breath and swung the ball down the lane in front of me. Not only did I hit some pins, but I got a strike. Everyone in the whole place cheered like crazy.

Except Dale.

He only said one thing. "I knew it was the shoes."

Dale and I met during my first week at college in 1987. We have supported each other through trials and triumphs and everything in between. There is something extraordinary about friendships that span more than half my life, but unless he works as one of my caregivers, Dale and I don't see each other all that much. I am at a place in my life where I would like to meet more people and socialize more often than I do currently. But, whoever I spend social time with at this point sort of has some big shoes to fill.

Even if they aren't bowling shoes...

Out of all the amazing people in my life, the ones that I am closest to tend to be the ones who take my disability in stride. My close friends know that there are lots of things that we do that will probably need to be accommodated. They accept that as a given, and we figure it out. I have said it before, but it bears repeating. When I give seminars to people about disability issues, one of the things that I often suggest is to treat people with disabilities like they don't have disabilities, and then do whatever is necessary to accommodate the disabilities they do have.

Let me take a minute to describe what I mean by that. I always appreciate when people see me as a person first, and my disability as secondary. When people with disabilities are treated like they don't have disabilities, the disability isn't the focus of the interaction. Make small talk. Ask the person with the disability how their day is going or tell them what you liked about the latest play put on at the local community theater.

When I suggest that people do whatever they can to accommodate a disability, I am saying that whatever needs to be done to "level the playing field" should be done quickly and efficiently. Does a table that a wheelchair user can comfortably roll under need to be brought into the room? Does a chair need to be removed at the end of a row in the audience so that a wheelchair user can enjoy a concert without blocking the aisle? Does someone with low vision need to be informed of the layout of the room? Can an interpreter be made available for someone who uses sign language? Do anything about the lights or sound at an event need to be adjusted so that a person with Post Traumatic Stress Disorder or epilepsy would be comfortable attending? Can whatever event that is happening be adapted somehow so the person with the disability can participate? First and foremost, ask the person with the disability what they most need.

In my experience, when needed accommodations are taken care of at the beginning of an event, I am more able to focus on participating in what is going on around me.

When I was a freshman in high school, I joined a sports team for people with cerebral palsy. Everything in me wanted to do well, but when it came to working out effectively I was as clueless as a mouse without a maze. At the urging of my health teacher, I made an appointment with the athletic director. His name was Coach Cripps. I was hoping that he might be able to give me a few pointers.

Icy prickles of anxiety flooded through me with such intensity that I was sure I had just swallowed Antarctica. Although I had been assured the man I was about to meet was very nice, I knew him only by reputation.

Our head high school football coach had more wins in his career than any other coach in our school district, and most Texans tend to treat high school football with the reverence of a religion, so when I entered his office in my wheelchair that day, I felt a little like Dorothy right before she met the wizard. My palms were sweaty, and for a few minutes there, I would have bolted if only I had the ability.

Then he entered the room. "Hello," he said, with a warm smile. His voice was gentle, soothing my nerves like hot tea on a sore throat, but I hadn't quite gotten over my fear. "How can I help you?" he asked as his eyes tried to meet mine. I looked at the floor.

"Hey Coach Cripps," I whispered as my voice shook uncontrollably, "I don't know if you know me (why would he?); I'm Lorraine. I just joined a sports team for people with cerebral palsy, and I really want to do well, but I am not sure how to work out effectively. I was wondering if you would consider writing out a list of exercises that I could follow sometime in the next few weeks, so I have a template as I start to work out." All my words came out in a rush.

"I would be happy to help, Lorraine," he said without the slightest hesitation. "Let me see what I can do... I'll get back to you soon, okay?"

"Thanks, Coach Cripps." My voice was a tad bit stronger now. "I would appreciate any suggestions you have for me."

The next day, after Coach Cripps presented me with a complete workout plan, he asked, "Lorraine, do you mind if I go through your workout with you as you are doing it?"

I was stunned. "Coach Cripps, that would be amazing. Thank you." I didn't know it then, but he would work with me as I trained at least once a day for the remainder of my high school career.

At first Coach Cripps worked out with me alone, but eventually he brought me into the weight room at the same time as some of the most popular football players. At the time, I didn't realize what he was doing. But he knew that if some of the varsity football players saw me trying to get stronger, they would cheer me on. When that came to be, my social life improved immeasurably. Eventually the football team was just as excited to see me accomplish my goals as I was to see them accomplish theirs. In terms of support, we were all on the same team.

No mentor has had a more significant, positive impact on my life than Coach Cripps. His guidance and compassion helped to shape who I am as a person. He was brilliant in many things, not the least of which was football. He knew what inclusion was all about.

**Accommodations**

There is a lot of talk about "reasonable accommodations" for people with disabilities in terms of employment. That is because the Americans with Disabilities Act, which was passed in 1990, has a section on employment and the accommodations that employers can make so that people with disabilities can comfortably do the job they were hired to do. Many sites online have lists of accommodation suggestions as well.

I am all about employment accommodations and think they are an important part of the ADA in bringing about equality in society. But I want to talk about a different kind of accommodation. The natural accommodations people make for me in everyday life. I call them casual accommodations. I believe that casual accommodations can make people with disabilities feel more included no matter what they happen to be doing.

- A friend of mine bought me a hands-free leash that I can put around my waist in my wheelchair so that my service dog and I can go for walks on the bike trail near our house by ourselves.

- For Christmas, a good friend of mine bought me several pairs of extra-long socks. She knows that my cerebral palsy prevents me from independently bending my knees, and therefore, my feet slip off the foot pedals of my wheelchair often. I use the tops of my socks as leverage sometimes to move my feet back in place. The extra-long socks make the whole process much easier.

- When I went to stay with a friend for a few days several years ago, she put a shoelace on the bathroom door knob for me. She was a former caregiver, and she knew that in my house, I have shoelaces on all the door knobs so that I can grab the shoelace as I am leaving the room and shut the door behind me independently. This woman did the same thing in her house so that I could maintain my privacy and dignity whenever I used her bathroom.

- I was spending a few hours at a friend's house before she drove me to a doctor's appointment. I found out that the night before, she had rearranged the living room furniture so that I would have more room to get around in my wheelchair.

- Another friend and I go to city commission meetings together on occasion. He has an SUV. Every time he puts my wheelchair in the back of his vehicle, he folds the seat down so that he doesn't have to take my wheelchair apart. Doing so means that I can get in and out of his car and into my chair quickly and easily.

- One of my friends actually built a ramp so that I can get into his house whenever I visit. He keeps it in the garage when not needed.

Here are some examples of how you can accommodate people with disabilities in your life.

- Do you want to invite your new coworker who happens to use a wheelchair to the potluck you are having this weekend? Ask her the best way to navigate the step at the front of your house. Be willing to recruit the neighbors or friends to help you, if necessary.

- You want to invite your sister and brother-in-law to spend a few days of the holidays at your house. Your brother-in-law was diagnosed with multiple sclerosis a few years ago, but you do not have an accessible shower with a shower chair. In a pinch, a lawn chair or a folding chair work well, if it can fit.

- You are at the grocery store and you see a young man who is a little person struggling to reach something on a shelf that is just out of his grasp. You offer to get it for him, and if he answers affirmatively, you take the item off the shelf and hand it to him so that he can drop it in his cart.

  The list of casual accommodations that can be made is potentially endless.

One of my favorite stories about accommodation comes from my former case manager, Amy.

She told me she was engaged to a wonderful guy named Jordan. Then she told me that she was getting married on October 5th. Since my birthday is the day before, I knew what day of the week that was.

"Wait," I said, a bit confused. "Isn't that a Monday?"

She laughed. "Yes."

My confusion remained until she explained the situation.

"Jordan was injured during his time in Iraq," she explained. "He was part of the Mobile-Maintenance unit, fixing vehicles of all sorts. There was a work accident that left him with severe brain damage and eight compressed disks, four in his neck and four in his back.

"Jordan's traumatic brain injury causes significant impairment with memory and concentration and is even more intense because he also has post-traumatic stress disorder. The combination of these diagnoses has impacted his daily functioning, especially in social, occupational, and educational realms. We decided to get married on October 5th because that is the day we officially started dating four years ago. Since Jordan gets frustrated with how difficult it is for him to remember things, we thought it would be a good idea to just keep the same date, to make life a little bit easier for him. . . ."

A few weeks later, she told me "We decided not to have much in the way of a ceremony because I did not want to overwhelm him on a day that was supposed to be solely full of joy. Our wedding day was quiet and low key but it was a truly wonderful day."

That just might be the most amazing accommodation I have ever heard of.

Natural accommodations don't have to be difficult, they just might have to be a bit outside the box. All it takes is the motivation for inclusion. Most casual accommodations are not difficult to implement. The best way to casually accommodate people with disabilities is to ask the person with the disability directly what it is they need.

I require some accommodations because of my physical disability, and I require some accommodations that are quite different because of my mental illness.

# Chapter 10

## My Mental Illness

When I talk about the issues that affect me psychologically, I tend to refer to them as my "psych issues" or my "psych diagnosis." Those terms feel a little softer to me than saying I am affected by a "mental illness." When I think of the latter term, movies like *One Flew Over the Cuckoo's Nest* and *Psycho* come to mind with their crazed characters intent on harming others due to their mental illness. But after I had written several drafts of this book, I realized that mental illness is a more common phrase, and tweaking a label isn't going to make me feel any different about the issues I deal with.

Mental illness is much more common than some people might think. According to the National Alliance on Mental Illness, or NAMI nearly 1 in 5 people in this country experience mental illness in a given year. Think about all the new moms who deal with postpartum depression or people who have legitimate fears and phobias based on some things they have been through. There are many people who struggle with varying degrees of anxiety or depression. There are lots of things people can be experiencing that could be defined as a mental illness.

The reason I am willing to talk about my mental illness openly is because I get tired of the stigma that surrounds mental illness in our society. It just doesn't make any sense to me. I mean seriously, when I go over to friends' houses to watch the Super Bowl it seems that every other commercial is about erectile dysfunction. If that issue can be openly discussed on national airways without many people raising so much as an eyebrow, why do people usually look like they have to go to the bathroom when I mention that I have a mental illness? It's hard for me to understand. My mental illness doesn't make me any more broken than my cerebral palsy does.

In several of my graduate school courses, there were discussions about the higher rate of anxiety and depression among people with disabilities than among the general population. That makes sense to me. Disability is not an easy thing to deal with. For me, some days are better than others when it comes to my ability to manage my moods. Sometimes I have a good few weeks, and sometimes all I can do is take things one day at a time. Sometimes one hour at a time. Or five minutes at a time. Whatever works.

In terms of what I disclose about my mental illness, I learned a long time ago not to tell too many people about the specifics of my diagnosis. In my experience, when people know the details, they tend to label me or generalize, or they go to the internet and get the wrong information. I hate that. When people get information about my mental illness from sources other than me, sometimes they get scared of my symptoms before they have experienced me having them. And I know there are some symptoms that will never come. In my experience, telling people my specific diagnosis tends to backfire badly.

Therefore, I am more willing to talk about all kinds of symptoms that I deal with and less about the diagnosis itself.

Even though the diagnosis came decades ago, talking about it can make me uncomfortable even now. I still worry that people won't get it. Or they will treat me differently, like I am nothing more than the mental illness I have. Just like the fact that I am a wheelchair user, it's another thing that potentially will make some people hesitate to be around me, and that can be discouraging. Episodes of emotional distress in my world are slowly getting fewer and farther between. And I know that is a good thing. I am slowly coming to terms with the fact that, as much as I wish it were different, my mental illness is never going to completely disappear. The best I can do is manage my symptoms to the best of my ability.

I see managing my symptoms to be very much like the way I imagine someone would manage diabetes. In that case, a person can monitor their diet, exercise often, and take all their medication at the appropriate times. And sometimes, despite their best efforts, their blood sugar is too high or too low anyway. Because that is the nature of their illness. Even if I use the skills and strategies that I have been taught to manage my mental illness perfectly, my emotions are still going to be out of whack sometimes. That is the nature of my illness, and not always in my control.

Since the issues surrounding mental illness affect me every day, it is vitally important to me that the people who are around me the most have a basic understanding of what they are. When that is the case, many parts of my life are much easier.

The question usually comes from good friends at a time when I am struggling. They want to know how to best help me.

What is it like to manage a mental illness?

It's like there is a dark cloud following me all the time. It isn't always directly overhead, and some days I don't even notice it. But it's always there, part of the landscape. At times, just waiting to swoop in.

On most days, all it means is that it's a little harder to be happy. Or maybe that I have to process some emotion before I can focus on today. It's the reason my reactions are on overdrive occasionally. My emotions can have the upper hand and overwhelm me. It is easy for me to blame myself for that.

Sometimes there is thunder that accompanies the dark cloud in the form of a trigger, and I can put on a raincoat and galoshes. I have been known to tell close friends what thunder sounds like to me. That way they can help me de-escalate when it rains. Sometimes storms hit me out of nowhere when I wasn't expecting to get wet. And then there are times when a monsoon has been known to put me out of commission for several days. At those times, I stay in bed under the covers and concentrate on breathing in and out because doing anything else feels like it is too much effort. That kind of thing does not happen very often.

It's not something I can "snap out of" or "get over." It's not that easy. And it doesn't help when people tell me to look on the bright side. Believe me, I put forth lots of effort to hold myself together the best that I know how. Sometimes a flashback from an event a long time ago completely rocks my world.

And the cloud is still there.

How can people support me?

Understand that I have a dark cloud following me. Don't be scared or awkward. It's just a cloud. It is simply one more thing in my life that I have to manage.

Don't put me in a box with a label. There are others who deal with a similar cloud, but I may respond to a particular situation in a completely different way from somebody else. Whenever there is thunder (a trigger), know that I hear it, even if nobody else can understand why it is such a big deal. And please be mindful enough not to create more thunder in my life when it can be avoided.

My dark cloud is unique to me. It doesn't belong to anyone else. And even if someone got rid of their dark cloud by doing a particular thing, it does not mean that the same remedy will work for me in the same way.

The cloud that follows me is part of my world. Sometimes it frustrates me because it makes my life harder. Sometimes it makes me sad because it colors how other people see me. Once some people have been told about the cloud, they run in another direction. There have also been numerous times over the years when people have blamed my being hurt on the cloud instead of taking responsibility for the things they have done that have caused me pain. That is not okay. Compassion is what I need more than anything.

I'm Lorraine.

I still laugh out loud and try not to take life too seriously.

I love wheelchair ballroom dancing.

Writing is one of my passions.

I prefer romantic comedies to science fiction movies.

My "made-on-the-stove" popcorn is legendary, I'm told.

Advocacy is part of my soul.

Road trips are the ultimate good time.

Sonic cherry limeades are the bomb.

Raisins make me gag. So do black olives and pimento cheese.

I love my job at the local magazine in my community. I write a column called Hometown Heroes. It means I get to meet great people on a regular basis and tell many other people about the good things that they do. What could be better than that?

Cuddling with my spectacular service dog is my favorite pastime.

Jigsaw puzzles used to challenge me. Not so much anymore. These days I tend to get bored if I can't find all the edge pieces right away.

The Little Drummer Boy will always be my favorite Christmas carol.

The West Wing is, in my opinion, the greatest television show of all time.

And I respectfully request that when we are together, you see all of me; don't let my mental illness "cloud" your judgment.

Remember the question that I talked about earlier that I get asked often? People want to know, if there were a pill that I could take to get rid of my disability, like it had never happened, would I take it? Let me take this opportunity to be a little more accurate. The answer is "no" on my physical disability, but I would take a pill to erase the existence of my mental illness in a heartbeat.

There are only certain ways my physical disability affects my life, whereas my mental illness can affect almost everything I do. In specific ways, it can affect every interaction that I have and most of the thoughts in my head. My mental illness is hard to get away from. But there are plenty of times I can easily forget that I use a wheelchair to get from point A to point B. My psychiatric symptoms, though, are not always as predictable. They fight with me often. Sometimes they win.

The following text is part of a blog post I wrote in an effort to describe what it feels like when I am having a bad day emotionally. I am speaking to my mental illness.

*Most of the time I can keep you at bay, just underneath the surface. Most people don't know your depth, strength, or intensity. If I can ask them how they are, you get deflected. I've become an expert at keeping you hidden. A smile. A laugh. Remembering a funny or heartwarming experience sometimes works. Distracting myself with a book or a movie is usually a last resort.*

*But the thing is, even with all the skills and strategies I have been taught, you never completely go away. It's like you are there waiting sometimes, for someone to hurt my feelings or for something not to go well when I was counting on it. In those situations, you can rear your ugly head and crash into my thoughts like sticky black goo, weighing me down and drowning out every morsel of positive energy that I try ferociously to hang on to. You knock the delicate balance of my emotions on its ass, and when I am off balance the heavy, sticky black goo goes everywhere. Left unchecked, it multiplies and becomes bigger than I am, some days leaving me feeling like I can't breathe and I fight to keep my head above water. Will it be too much this time? Will I drown?*

Most days are a combination of good and stressful. That is probably true for most people.

## Abandonment

One way that my mental illness manifests in my life is that I have an incredibly intense fear of abandonment. That means that most of the time I am terrified that I am going to end up alone. Or maybe more specifically in recent years, that I will end up alone in a nursing home a long time before I am ready to be there.

The thought scares the spit out of me, to the point that whenever somebody I care about leaves my life, even if it's for a completely legitimate reason, I am convinced it means that I did something wrong, and they would have stayed if I had done something differently. I feel like I am being abandoned. Logically, I know better. My emotions are a different story entirely.

When I watch various friends around me, it becomes clear quickly that most other people have an understanding that most of the time, people are in our lives on a temporary basis. You enjoy them while you can, and then a neighbor or a friend gets a job in a new city, or there is a wedding, graduation, or some other major event that call people away. And for most people, while it is sad that relationships change and often experience growing pains, they view it as a natural part of life.

For me, that kind of thing can be devastating.

The loss and grief I experience every time one of my significant relationships ends can be overwhelming. It can feel like I am suffocating. Like I can't breathe. To me, abandonment is one of the loneliest and most terrifying experiences there is. It can feel like part of my soul is dying. And I can't remember a time when it wasn't a part of my emotional world.

Nobody can tell me why this intense fear of abandonment started with any degree of certainty, but I have my theories.

I know the following story only in the retelling.

In the predawn hours of an early fall day, the chill in the air was both outside and inside the walls of that stark, barren hospital. The medical team had been assembled unexpectedly. I had let my mom know that I was making my way into the world ten weeks early, and my dad was so caught off guard when she woke him up to tell him, he thought it had to be a false alarm.

In the delivery room, I made my presence known with a cry that shook every ounce of my barely three-pound body. Because my lungs had not developed enough for me to breathe on my own, I was quickly placed in an incubator and given supplemental oxygen. I was given medical tests and monitors and stayed in the ICU for the next seven weeks.

What I wasn't given was affection.

Apparently, the environment was sterile in a myriad of ways. My parents tell me that I was in a room with other preemie babies throughout that time, and they could look at me through a window for exactly fifteen minutes. At 7 p.m. every day, they would stand on the other side of the window, and nurses would raise the blinds for them to look in. At exactly 7:15, the blinds were lowered until they came back the next day. They weren't allowed to be alone with me, cuddle with me or touch me in any way. If any of the preemie babies on the unit were not doing well at that time in an evening, the blinds stayed down with no explanation. Mom and dad were told to go home. For the first seven weeks of my life, whether my parents saw me on a given day was hit or miss, and the only touch I ever received was strictly for medical purposes.

As I consider that reality, I have often wondered if those circumstances had a lasting effect on who I am today. Bouts of depression affect me routinely, and my issues of abandonment are sometimes beyond intense. Can those issues be connected to my environment in the weeks following my birth? It is something I will probably never know for sure, but the thought squirms restlessly in my mind with a frequency that says it's simply not settled.

Unlike in years past, parents of preemies nowadays are encouraged to spend a lot of time in the NICU with their babies.

Even if they can't be held, contemporary incubators often have built-in gloves, so parents can lovingly caress their babies while they receive the care they need. In fact, it seems like the environment for premature babies today is pretty much the opposite of what it was when I was born. It is the parents who spend most of the time with their children, and medical staff comes by in fifteen-minute increments to do what they need to do.

I cannot express the hope it gives me to know that the needs of premature babies today are seen with a drastically different perspective than they were when I was an infant. I must say that I think today's practices are infinitely better than the ones that were used years ago.

Since I don't remember a time when I haven't struggled with abandonment issues, I work very hard to improve this area of my life. I get a lot of practice because about 90 percent of the time, the only people I interact with during a day are my caregivers. And about 95 percent of the time, caregivers are only with me for a few months or so.

When people move out of my life, it hits me much harder than most. When I am triggered badly with feelings of abandonment the only way I can describe what I am feeling is that there is a gaping hole inside me that simply can't be filled because I am terrified that I won't ever deeply connect with anyone long term. And every time people move on from my life, it can be overwhelming to know that I have to try and make connections with other people all over again. Decades ago, I was known to be clingy and needy in most of my relationships, and those behaviors only resulted in the opposite of what I wanted. although I can say that I am much better these days, I am still a work in progress and am committed to doing the deeply challenging work required to improve in this area of my life.

The blog post that follows describes some of the ways my mental illness affects me currently.

It's a complicated issue. Stay with me.

These days, my abandonment issues sometimes come out in quirky ways. Every once in a while, when a caregiver asks to work fewer hours or takes a vacation, I have been known to tear up. Or when a caregiver that I am close to has three days off in a row, I have been known to panic because, in an irrational moment of fear, I have convinced myself that they will not come back and they never liked me to begin with. I do my best to shield my caregivers when thoughts like this run through my head. These are my issues. And most of the time working for me is, after all, just a job to them.

One of the things that complicates this issue is the fact that I need to surround myself with caregivers to get my physical needs met, and I am aware that the position of caregiver has one of the highest turnover rates of any job in the country. Another thing that makes this issue complicated is that I must ask my caregivers to help me with the most intimate physical things that I do. And it is difficult to have emotional boundaries with caregivers when I can't have any physical ones. Additionally, since I don't drive, most days, caregivers are the only people I see. I become much more attached to them than they do to me.

This is not my favorite part of who I am, but I also know I can't help it. And I often must remind myself that, in the same way that I can't blame myself for having cerebral palsy, it is not my fault I have a mental illness either.

This aspect of my personality is often misunderstood, and I sincerely get that. If I had a broken arm that required special care, it would be easy to explain to those who are around me.

So what do I do?

When I have a caregiver that I am particularly fond of, I ask them to stay in touch with me on some level when they stop working. Sometimes they offer. I let them know that I don't have any expectation that they will be a major emotional support in my life. Rather, what I mean is that I would sincerely appreciate an email or a text message from time to time, just to let me know how they are.

I don't keep in contact with most of the caregivers I have worked with after their employment with me ends, but there are those gems who are few and far between that understand me when I tell them:

It's a complicated issue. Stay with me.

In whatever capacity, for as long as you can.

I, along with several quality professional counselors I have worked with, will tell you that my mental illness doesn't mean that I am crazy. Rather, my diagnosis means that my emotions can be intense sometimes, and that my emotional response to a situation may seem more extreme than what would make sense to an outsider looking in.

**Sometimes I get overwhelmed.**

Let me try and explain it this way. When I go out in public with one of my caregivers, and someone tries to get information about me only from my caregiver while pretending that I am not in the room, I am going to be angry. The thing is, that anger is not going to be exclusively about the situation at hand. Instead, on some level, I am reminded in that situation of how many hundreds or thousands of times the same thing has happened before over the course of many years. My reaction has more to do with all of them collectively.

**And sometimes I experience triggers.**

Triggers can affect me on less than stellar days. This is the "thunder" I was referring to earlier. A sound or a smell or the way someone says something, even it is unintentional, can remind me of something traumatic I've been through, to the point that it can feel like I am experiencing it again. Some triggers are mild, and some are massive. Most fall somewhere in between the two.

I have done enough "self-awareness" work, as I like to call it, to identify what most of my triggers are, and that is the information I choose to share with the people who are around me the most. Some of my biggest triggers include people taking my power or choices away from me, people giving me the message that my feelings and needs don't matter, and people treating me in ways other than how they would treat a competent adult.

**It's okay not to know what to say or what to do. All I ask is that you don't let your feelings of helplessness turn into fear or blame.**

So how can people help me the most? Just be with me in the moment.

When I am having a hard time, I don't expect anyone to fix anything for me. In fact, when I am emotional, I would rather people not make suggestions about how to "fix" the situation that is making me upset. Instead, when I am experiencing intense emotion, a kind word or a hug speaks volumes. Those kinds of things say, "I am here, and I care." That is what I need to know the most.

Sometimes, when I am feeling overwhelmed with a situation, it might seem like I am overreacting. I happen to have a unique philosophy about "overreaction." I don't think it is possible.

People are responding to the feelings inside of them. If those feelings are intense, the reaction will be as well. Someone telling me that I am overreacting comes across to me as dismissive. You may not understand why my reaction is so intense and therefore need me to explain it, but that doesn't mean my reaction is not valid.

I have good and bad days, and on rare occasions, I lose it. I am willing to bet that most people can say that. Those closest to me have said that in their experience with me, my emotions can be a little more intense than they would imagine the emotions of other people would be, but my emotional reactions to things are not inappropriate.

**From experience, I can say that at the times I am the most emotional, I need compassion instead of judgment.**

Other people are absolutely entitled not to agree with my point of view; it is just probably best not to state that you have a different opinion when I am highly emotional. Wait until I have had a chance to calm down, and we can have a rational conversation.

Several years ago, at home on a Saturday, I was not having a good day emotionally. I was totally overwhelmed with several issues that happened to be going on in my life. As I always do, I told my caregiver where I was in my head, just so she would be aware. A couple hours later, in the middle of her shift, I let myself cry. As the tears were still streaming down my face, my caregiver looked at me and said, "I really think you do this to yourself. You are simply upsetting yourself."

Let me be clear, having this caregiver blame me for being overwhelmed did not help me in the slightest. In fact, it only made me want to cry harder. It felt like she was kicking me when I was down. It was obvious this caregiver did not understand that as I was struggling, her support would have helped me tremendously. At a time when I was already significantly emotional, getting blamed for the symptoms of my mental illness didn't make any part of the situation easier.

**What could have happened differently:**
On an otherwise quiet afternoon, I am not having a good day emotionally. When she sees my tears, my caregiver lets me know that she understands that I am having a hard time today. She lets me know that she wants to support me and is willing to help me do whatever would make me feel better.

In a similar situation recently, the person who was with me responded completely differently. One morning, the lights would not turn on in two rooms of my house. My first thought was that I had blown a fuse. I called my friend Andrea and asked her to come over because I cannot reach the breaker box in my storage room. After she got here, she fiddled with switches for a while without success and then called her father-in-law, a retired electrician. After trying several things, he couldn't come up with a solution and thought that I might have a wiring problem. After he left, I started to freak out a bit. Visions of rewiring work that would cost thousands of dollars were taunting me.

Andrea has known me for a long time and recognized when I started to panic. She looked me directly in the eye while she gently and reassuringly put her hand on my arm. "I know some of the possibilities for a fix are expensive. Let's wait and see what we are dealing with. We will get through whatever we need to." Then she called various wiring companies and explained the issue in detail, because I was a bit too emotional in those few minutes to do that on my own.

Andrea's calm attitude and validation made me want to be calm as well. I took several deep breaths and reminded myself not to panic because I didn't yet know all the details.

The problem turned out to be that something had melted within an outlet by my bed. It was an easy fix for the guy from the wiring company, and I only got charged the cost of a weekend service call. The situation could have been far worse.

---

**What she did right:**

Andrea noticed quickly that my stress level was rising and immediately started to do things that she knew were effective for me, like validating my feelings and giving me reassurance through her words and her touch. She also reminded me not to panic before I knew all the facts, and that whatever the outcome, I was not alone. At no point during our interaction did Andrea blame me for my reaction or make me feel bad in any way. Instead, she simply let me know she was supportive and on my side.

---

## When I am emotional, I do not respond well to people who tell me to calm down.

I am not sure any person on the planet has ever responded positively when someone has told them to calm down. In my experience, hearing that is the opposite of helpful. My emotions cannot be turned on and off like a switch, and if some situation has resulted in my being emotional, my calming down is a process. Therefore, telling me to calm down and expecting me to get back to "normal" in a matter of minutes or seconds is like asking me to go outside and climb a tree. I have a disability that simply prevents me from doing so. And I cannot help that. Even though I wish that I could.

I am completely aware that the mental illness that I deal with is mine alone. It is up to me to learn how to manage my symptoms in a way that works for me. It is not anyone else's responsibility to make sure that I don't feel abandoned or that I never have any triggers. It isn't up to anyone else to "fix" me. I just sincerely appreciate it when people are supportive when I happen to be experiencing some symptoms. Other people are responsible for their choices (like telling me they would keep in touch with me and not following through).

Before I had the skills and strategies to manage my emotions that I do now, there got to be a point many years ago, when I knew that what people saw on the outside was not my authentic self. I didn't want to cry or get angry on a whim. I didn't want the people who were around me to feel bad about themselves at the end of our interaction. I knew that the behaviors that I was displaying were not who I was in my heart. That is when I knew it was time to start going to counseling.

At my local mental health center, I had the honor of working with an extraordinarily gifted counselor for a long time. George was warm and compassionate and got to know me very well. We met for appointments every week for eleven years. It was George who introduced me to the concept of mindfulness, which means doing your best to be fully present in the current moment. It turns out when you put that concept into practice, it is much more difficult to get lost in memories of the past or anxieties about the future. Mindfulness is very helpful for me.

He also taught me some "self-soothing" techniques. When I am having a bad day or a bad hour, going out on the bike trail near my house to breathe in the fresh air or listening to some music I like can ground me in the reality that there are lots of good things in my life. Whenever I am experiencing abandonment issues, he suggested that I touch something that feels good, like a soft blanket or a favorite pillow. He thought that if I could put my arms around something like that, I could lessen the force of feeling all alone. When I remember to do it, I have found that it works. My feelings of abandonment don't disappear completely, but they do lose some of their intensity.

What I like about all those techniques is that I can utilize them on my own, and I am not dependent on anybody else to make them happen. I just like people around me to have an awareness of some of the issues I deal with, so if my symptoms happen to surface, nobody is caught completely off guard. But I am the only one responsible for managing my illness.

My physical and psychiatric disabilities sort of play off each other. If I am having a bad day emotionally, chances are good that my pain and spasms will be severe. If I am not moving well physically, it is harder for me to be in a great mood.

I don't have these issues on purpose. I promise. I don't know of anyone who would choose to deal with them.

If there is a silver lining to my dealing with these issues, I would say that they have made me much more emotionally aware than I probably would have been without them. It is easy these days for me to recognize emotions not only in myself but also to be more sensitive to the emotions people around me are experiencing. I concentrate on listening to what is going on with the people I care about and try to offer compassion without judgment, which is the same thing I ask of the people around me. The issues I deal with have made me keenly aware that everyone else has their own.

One of my biggest supports when I am experiencing my mental illness is my service dog, Leah. She helps me in many ways that are both physical and emotional.

# Chapter 11

## Service Dogs

I was introduced to the world of service dogs in October of 1998 when I was matched with my first service dog, Marshall, a big yellow lab with a stubborn, ornery streak (like me) and an enormous heart. We bonded instantly. Marshall loved to play, but once he got his service dog harness on, he was all business. We had almost nine wonderful years together before cancer returned a third time. Dr. Tom (my vet) and I made the decision to put Marshall to sleep the day after I got back from the Ms. Wheelchair America pageant.

The process of applying for a service dog is rather intense. There is a long application, and everyone must submit a video detailing their disability and explaining why they believe a service dog would be good for them. Based on the information received in the application and the video, the staff matches specific people with specific dogs. When I got Leah, I had to fill out an application, but I didn't have to make a video, since I had a service dog previously. At the time of my second application for a dog, the fact that I previously had Marshall also moved me up on the waiting list.

When people are accepted into the program, they go to the dog school and train for about two weeks. That is where the owners learn all the commands the dogs know, and a huge amount of time is spent working together and deeply connecting.

For me, the bonds with both my dogs began the minute that I met them. And even after eighteen years of having service dogs in my life, the bonds that are between us are still hard for me to describe.

As a person with a disability, I have often said that I long for a world where people with disabilities are equals. Where there is no discrimination, no struggle. A place where strengths are focused on rather than weaknesses, and I am seen as a person before my wheelchair is part of the equation.

That world has been a reality every time I have interacted with my dogs. They don't care about disability. They see me exactly as I am.


*Hi Everyone,*

*This is Leah, Lorraine's black lab service dog.*

*I asked her if I could write for a bit because I wanted to tell you what our life together is like.*

*Lorraine and I have been together for more than nine years now. Our first full day together was her first day in her new house and it was also her fortieth birthday. That was a big day for both of us. I was just shy of a year old at the time.*

*I came from a dog service training school named CARES in Concordia, Kansas, and I was bred to be a service dog to help people with disabilities.*

*After spending my first eight weeks at CARES I was moved to a prison in Colorado with some of my siblings. I was raised by an inmate there, and he and I spent the better part of my first year together. I was taught basic commands and how to socialize with both other dogs and people. Prisoners only get to train puppies as part of a reward program if they are model prisoners, so the prisoner that trained me had to earn the right to do so.*

*When Lorraine went to visit the prison where some of the dogs from CARES were trained, she asked one of the prisoners in the program why he trained dogs when he knew that he would eventually have to give them away. His answer stuck with her. He said, "Lorraine, I am in here because I was selfish. I train dogs for people with disabilities because I want to give back to society and make life better for a few people in the process." Tears welled up in Lorraine's eyes when he said that. I thought it was pretty cool myself, although I don't cry if I can help it. Instead, I sighed with contentment at the sweetness of the sentiment.*

*I am from the Harry Potter litter. All the litters of service dogs are named according to a theme, so the school can keep track of health concerns that run within the families of puppies and that kind of thing. My real name is Luna, after Luna Lovegood, but Lorraine didn't like that character in the story of Harry Potter because she was kind of spacey. So she asked Sarah, the owner of the school, if she could change my name. Sarah told Lorraine that I needed the L at the beginning of my name and the A at the end for us to be consistent with training, so on the second day we were together Lorraine changed my name to Leah, and we have never looked back.*

*We were in training together for two full weeks. We walked in a circle about a bazillion times around a gym, so I could get used to Lorraine's wheelchair and always being on her left side. I can't be on the right because when we are at Target or Walmart or a grocery store and we go to check out, all the candy treats and the things I am not supposed to have are on the right.*

*We don't want me to be tempted unnecessarily. That could be bad news for everyone.*

*It was also during training that Lorraine and I bonded, and she told me she would always take care of me. I liked hearing that, but I take good care of Lorraine, too. I can sense quickly when Lorraine is upset or frustrated, and I do a good job of calming her down. I can do that better than almost anybody else.*

*I'm not braggin' or nothin'. It's just true.*

*When she is having a bad time, I hop up by her wheelchair and put my two front paws in her lap. That is my "It's time to hug me" pose. I wait for her to snuggle with me, and if I don't think one hug did the trick, I rest for a second and then put my two front paws on her lap again. I make sure she keeps hugging me until she feels better. Then I usually go back to sleep until the next time she needs me.*

*Sometimes I pick things up when Lorraine drops them. That's one of the things I was trained to do. Some days, I am just not feeling it though. On certain days, if Lorraine drops something and asks me to go get it, I think it's mine. That's logical, right? Don't the "finders keepers" and "possession is 90 percent of the law" rules apply here? Thought so.*

*Don't worry, I usually give it back after a while. Lorraine's old cell phone had lots of my teeth marks in it, though. I had a hard time giving that up whenever I got a hold of it.*

*The last time that we went to our vet, Dr. Tom told us that I gained a little weight. So one of Lorraine's friends bought her a hands-free leash that she wraps around her belly, making both hands available to guide her wheelchair. For the last few weeks she has taken me for a long walk every day on the bike trail in her power chair.*

*Yesterday, right after we had started out, we had a big black lab follow us. He was into me. Just sayin'. We were a little intimidated at first, so we tried to go in front of him. He wasn't going to have it. Every time we tried, he would run to catch up. After a few minutes, Lorraine noticed that he had a collar with a tag on, so we realized that he must just be lost. He finished our walk with us, all the while trying to sniff my butt. I, on the other hand, was playing hard to get. I needed him to know that I am just not that kind of girl.*

*After the walk, he looked kind of hot so we invited him in for a drink. (No. Not that kind of hot and no, not that kind of drink!) He was growing on me, and I didn't even protest when he drank from my water bowl.*

*Lorraine thought that was very hospitable of me. It even trans-lated into an extra milk bone. Score!*

*While our new doggy friend rested, Lorraine looked at his tag and found the number for his owner. We ran around and played while we waited for his owner to pick him up. Right before he left, he peed all over the living room floor, but overall, we had a nice afternoon together.*

*After he was gone, I reminded Lorraine that he was the one who peed on the floor (just in case she was confused) and asked when I could see him again. I'm starting to have a little crush. BOW WOW WOW! Is this what they call puppy love?*

*Anyway, I like being Lorraine's partner. She says that we both do better when we are together, and she is right. I am fiercely protective of her, and I make sure she knows that even though lots of caregivers who are college students come and go in our lives, we are a family. She often tells me that I love her differently than most people. I'm not quite sure what she means by that, but I know I've always seen her abilities and not much else. Lorraine also appreciates that I am a "bitch" (apparently, that is what a female dog is called) in description only. She gives good belly rubs, and she understands when I tell her my four biggest priorities in life.*

*Feed me*

*Walk me*

*Love me*

*Naps*

*For me, wiggling my whole body is second nature when it is time to fill my tummy. I LIKE that kibble!*

*I think I'll stop typing now. My paws are getting kind of tired. If you see us out in public, please remember to ask Lorraine if you can pet me before you do so. When I have my harness on, I am working.*

*For now, woof, and have a doggone good day!*

*Leah*

Leah has no expectations about anything I should be doing differently. No preconceived ideas about my worth. All she wants from me is love and kibble. In return, she (and Marshall) have taught me the true meaning of unconditional love. Whenever the world has made me feel "less than," it's my dogs who have made me feel "enough." My dogs have added a whole new dimension of "goodness" to my life.

Late at night we have deep conversations, and I tell her everything that is in my heart and soul. She trained herself to hold my hand, and in her unique way, she reassures me that the two of us belong together and all is well. She is unquestionably my best friend. Let's just say that it is probably a good thing that she cannot talk. Leah keeps all my secrets.

As a service dog, under the Americans with Disabilities Act, Leah can go anywhere that I go in public. That is a good thing because the two of us like to be together.

**Some service dog rules:**

Some people say that it is never okay to pet a service dog. I have always learned that it is up to the owner whether he or she feels comfortable with a service dog being petted. I will say this:

**Always ask permission before you pet a service dog.**

A few years ago, I was sitting in a fast food restaurant in my neighborhood with one of my caregivers. We were engrossed in our conversation. Marshall, my first service dog was with me, and as he always did in public, he was wearing his harness so that other people would know that he was, in fact, a service dog who was working at the time. I gave him the down-stay command, and he lay down at my feet.

Out of nowhere, a little girl, about three years old, came up from behind us and basically tackled Marshall without warning. My dog was incredibly sweet, so he didn't snap at her, but her actions caught him off guard. He was frightened and looked to me for reassurance. He had been distracted from his job of making sure that I was okay.

The only thing this little girl's mom said to me was, "She just loves dogs!"

I am fully aware that this little girl meant no harm. But trained, harnessed service dogs in public are working, and at all times, their attention should only be on their owner.

**What could have happened differently:**
When the little girl sees Marshall in a restaurant, one of her parents asks my permission before letting her pet him. That way, they give me the choice as to whether touching my dog was okay with me in that moment. Their taking time to ask me first alerts Marshall to their presence, so that he is not startled when he is touched.

In the same way that I use my wheelchair because I have a disability, I also have a service dog because I have a disability. So, just like you probably wouldn't like a stranger tugging on your coat without any interaction, I don't like people touching my wheelchair or my service dog without checking with me first.

**The bond between a service dog and their owner should never be underestimated. It's not okay to leave a service dog at home because "other people will be there to help."** Numerous times over the past few years, before certain people in my life knew me well, they would suggest that we do something social and leave my service dog at home. To them, the logic was simple. "If other people are going to be with you to do what you need, then you don't need your service dog with you."

That isn't the way that it works. Service dogs are trained to increase the independence of their owners. Part of the reason I need mine with me is so that I don't have to ask anyone for help. And the less I have to ask for help, the more chance there is of people focusing on me as a person and not on my disability. That is always going to be what I want. So even though it might be an inconvenience for some people to have my service dog accompany us wherever we are going, if she is with me, I am more comfortable being who I am. Sometimes it is easier to face the world when she is by my side.

The only exception to having a service dog with me is if I decide it is better for them if they stayed home. I would never take them to a concert. (It would be too loud.) I would never take them to the zoo. (They could rile up the other animals and potentially create an unsafe situation for staff there.)

Whether I take my service dog with me anywhere should be entirely my call. It is appropriate to ask me to provide old sheets to put on the back seat of someone's car, or to ask that my dog sit in the back of the car instead of up front with me. I even have a good friend who happens to have a severe allergy to dog hair, and the two of us have always found ways to travel with my dog that work. It's not okay for anyone to ask me to leave my dog at home because doing so would be more convenient for them.

The bonds between service dogs and their partners with disabilities typically run deep and are very important. Service dogs promote independence in various ways.

Service dogs are only one subject that people ask me questions about.

# Chapter 12

## Frequently Asked Questions

### If I am sitting next to a wheelchair user, should I remain seated when everyone else stands up?

You should do whatever makes you feel comfortable. I never want to push my disability on anyone else, so I don't tend to ask people to sit in a room full of people who are standing. But if you feel better keeping your seat, that is a good thing too.

### Should I hold a door open for a wheelchair user?

The best bet is to ask the wheelchair user if he or she would like the door held open. If the answer is affirmative, then by all means, do so.

### How can I be respectful of your wheelchair as part of your personal space?

Never crowd a wheelchair user. Their wheelchair and other devices for mobility such as canes or a walker should be considered an extension of their space. This is also important because shifting in a wheelchair or doing a transfer often requires extra room. **Never push a wheelchair without asking permission to do so first.**

### If I see someone with a disability being disrespected, should I say something?

That depends. If the person with the disability is advocating on their own behalf and getting the results they desire, then I say don't interfere. If, on the other hand, the person with the disability is not getting results, ask if he or she would like assistance. Based on the answer you receive, respond accordingly.

## How do you feel about people without disabilities using automatic doors or going into accessible stalls in the bathroom?

I do not agree with anyone using automatic doors or accessible stalls in a bathroom simply for their personal convenience all the time. However, if on a rare occasion, someone has their hands full, I have no problem with them using an automatic door.

I get it. You have been shopping all day at the mall. You are carrying a million shopping bags and your large purse. You suddenly realize you have to pee. You enter the bathroom, and the stall closest to the door happens to be the accessible one. There is more room in there to put down everything you have been holding so that you can tend to the business at hand.

If there is nobody with a disability waiting, go ahead and use the accessible stall. Just get out as quickly as you can so that it is available as soon as possible to those who cannot use the other stalls.

## Why does it upset me when someone uses accessible parking who doesn't need it?

Throughout my life, I have had various friends who are wheelchair users. Some drove vans. A universal frustration to these friends is when someone who is driving a car parks in a van-accessible spot, and does not leave them enough room to get the lift down. Are you familiar with the "turtle on its back" concept? I have witnessed the major frustration these friends experience when they cannot finish their errands because someone else has parked where they shouldn't.

The other accessible parking issue that irritates me is when people use it for convenience. Yes, most accessible parking spots are close to an entrance. There is a reason for that and it is not to make things easier for the public at large. On several occasions, I have had someone who admits to being perfectly fit come up to me in a parking lot and ask, "Did I take your spot?" Then, without skipping a beat, they say something like, "It's okay, I'm just going into the store for five minutes."

Seriously?

The bottom line is, accessible spots are designated for drivers with disabilities that need them. If that is not you, then don't park there. Period.

**Is it appropriate to assume you understand someone's disability simply by reading their medical chart?**

In a word, no. A medical chart might give you the basics or a label, but only the person affected by the disability can tell you how they experience the disability. Listening to the person retains their humanity. Sometimes humanity can be lost when a chart is the only point of reference.

**How do you feel about receiving government benefits?**

I utilize the assistance of several government benefit programs. That does not make me lazy, and I don't do so by choice. If I had the stamina and the stability in my health, I would love to be working 40 hours per week and some overtime. Although I am sincerely grateful for the support that I receive, I didn't plan to be in the situation I am in.

Currently, I rely on government programs like Social Security Disability payments and food stamps to get by.

When I was a little girl, and people asked me what I wanted to do when I grew up, I NEVER looked up at them with big brown eyes and said that I wanted to live on government assistance for many years. Not many people aspire to receive SSI or SSDI payments, I promise. Not many people on welfare want to be. I do work at a couple of jobs, and I work very hard at what I do. I work as much as my disability allows me to. And I receive government benefits as well. Some people with disabilities cannot work at all. And there is nothing wrong with that.

With rare exception, government employees who oversee programs like food stamps and disability payments routinely treat me like I am "less than." I can call a government office and simply be inquiring about the status of my case (because I must reapply for benefits every year) and be sarcastically told, "I don't know, Lorraine, I'll get to it when I get to it." Sometimes after a statement like that, the worker will hang up on me. That is discouraging when collectively these programs sustain much of my livelihood. Just because I need that kind of help should not mean it is okay for anybody to be disrespectful.

Lots of people get help from the government, including all kinds of young people who take out student loans and grants in order to get an education. There should be no shame associated with reaching out for help when you truly need to—for anyone.

**I saw someone using a wheelchair, and it did not look like they needed to. Is that appropriate?**

First, I would encourage anyone to be careful about making assumptions until you know all the facts. There are many invisible disabilities that can take away a person's energy. Diabetes. Lupus. Fibromyalgia. A heart condition. And the list goes on. Just because someone does not have a physically obvious disability does not mean that their use of a wheelchair is inappropriate.

**How do I support someone with a mental illness who is going through a hard time?**

Be present, even if you cannot be there physically. Listen. Encourage. Be gentle. Be kind. Be patient. Communicate in various ways that you want to be on their side and they are not alone.

**If I see someone with a disability struggling, and I think there is a better way to accomplish what they are trying to do, should I suggest my idea?**

Ask the person with the disability if they would like the suggestion. If the answer is yes, then give it. Be okay if they still want to do things the way that they are used to.

**What do I do if I think I might have said something offensive to a person with a disability?**

I am well aware that with rare exception, people don't mean to be offensive. And I never want anyone to hesitate to communicate because they fear they might say the wrong thing. So please do not stress. Chances are good that, even if something came across in a way other than it was intended, no major harm was done.

In my case, if something comes across to me as offensive, I will gently let the person know. My favorite way to have people approach that kind of thing is to ask me "Is saying XYZ appropriate, or is there a word or phrase that you consider to be more respectful?"

**I've been hanging out with a person with a disability for a while, and I am starting to find them attractive. What do I do?**

First, make sure they are not dating someone else already. Then make your move.

**Is it appropriate to sit in someone's wheelchair when they are not in it?**

With permission. On a case-by-case basis.

**Is it appropriate to sit on a wheelchair user's lap?**

That is a pretty intimate gesture having to do with personal space. It is a personal preference. It also depends on age. Holding a baby on my lap is very different to having someone a few years older than me sit there. Always ask permission first.

**How can I best help if someone falls out of their wheelchair?**

Ask if they are okay and if they need more help than you can give them. Ask if they need you to call 911. If not, ask them to specifically tell you step by step how you can best be of assistance. Make sure you both understand the whole process before you begin to help get them off the floor.

**Is it okay to talk to, or invite, a person with a disability to activities that a person with a disability cannot participate in?**

Sometimes I like to watch baseball or basketball. I am never going to participate in those sports. It is okay to talk about anything as long as the person with the disability is engaged in the conversation.

**What should I tell my child about disability?**

I like to introduce the concept that people are more the same than different to kids. They are usually good at coming up with ways that people are all the same, as well as some things that make each of us unique. Remind kids that disability is not scary, it is merely a difference. And that disability is a difference, not a weakness.

**I have had some bad experiences interacting with people with disabilities in the past. Now I am a little gun-shy. How can I overcome that?**

People with disabilities, just like everyone else, have been known to have bad days. Sometimes we snap at people who don't deserve it. Sometimes we are less than kind. Keep in mind that one or two bad experiences do not equal the whole. Saying all people with disabilities are angry is like saying all blonds have more fun. It just isn't true. So give it another try. I bet you won't always be disappointed.

**My older relative just said something offensive about people with disabilities. What should I say to her?**

Different generations approach disability differently. Many years ago, it was socially acceptable to call people with disabilities "cripples" or "invalids." People do what they know. A gentle reminder that those terms are not used anymore, as well as some examples of what would be empowering language, would be a good response.

**One of my friends just got diagnosed with a disability. I want to be supportive. How can I do that?**

Everything you ever liked about your friend is still as true now as it was before you heard about the diagnosis. Remind your friend that you don't see him or her any differently, and that you want to be available during difficult times.

**I want to go to an event with my friend who is a wheelchair user. I am not sure if the location is accessible. What do I do?**

Call the location and talk to someone who works there. After talking to your friend who is a wheelchair user to know what the needs are, ask if the location can accommodate those needs.

**Do you think it is possible for someone to completely accept their disability?**

I think acceptance of anything that affects a person's life on a long-term basis is a process. Some days that process is easier than others. I also believe that everybody has their own way of dealing with their circumstances.

Speaking personally, I accept my disability today much more than I did when I was younger. On the days when I am stiff and in pain, it is harder to be positive about my circumstances, but that doesn't mean that I don't accept what they are. Disability doesn't define me, but it has shaped who I am, and I am okay with that.

# Chapter 13

## I'm Okay With Who I Am

When I was a senior in high school, I was in a kick-ass creative writing class. The woman who taught it had also taught me junior English, and I liked her immensely. In fact, thanks to Facebook, we are still in touch today. We have always had a nice connection. One of the things I thoroughly enjoyed about this class were the interesting writing assignments. Every student had started a journal at the beginning of the semester, and twice a week or so, we were given a new topic to explore in our writing. One such topic resonated with me to such an extent that I remember it clearly more than thirty years later.

As we entered class one morning, the message on the blackboard told us to start writing in our journals. We were to write about something we hated by completing the following sentence and explaining why. "I would hate you somewhat less if. . ."

It was the perfect opportunity to write about all the frustration caused by my disability.

Back then, my cerebral palsy was a bully—tough and mean—that tangled with my body and caused me pain and spasm. But it affected me so much more than physically. It was only because I was a wheelchair user that I could not fit under any of the tables in the cafeteria. So, I sat by myself, backing my wheelchair up against a huge brick pillar that was the only thing wide enough to accommodate my mode of transportation.

More painful to my heart, though, was my perceived idea that my cerebral palsy caused my isolation. Like all teenagers, I wanted to fit in and have a place among the "cool" crowd. I was lonely, and I longed to belong. But most of my peers at the time magnified my differences, and on numerous occasions, specific things happened that made me believe how much I wasn't one of "them." That is what kids do sometimes. Cerebral palsy sneered and hissed.

Late at night it always seemed to whisper: "You can't go for a run like most people. You can't even drive. I'll always make you different."

A few months after I started high school, I got involved in sports. I lifted weights. I worked out hard. Flying around the track gave me a sense of power and control. It was only over time that I realized that I would not be excelling in sports if I didn't have a disability. I was a teenager who was shy and quite awkward. If I didn't have a disability, I most likely would have spent my free time in the library rather than on the track.

Cerebral palsy was watching closely, taking it all in, but staying quiet.

In my first job after college, I learned some advocacy skills. It became clear to me soon after that I could use those skills to not only help myself but be a voice for others with disabilities who could not tell their stories on their own. On numerous occasions, I had the opportunity to go to the state capitol and give testimony to senators and representatives about programs that would be beneficial for those of us with disabilities.

A few years later, I was lucky enough to be on the state committee that designed a program that enabled people with disabilities to work without losing their eligibility for the state to pay their caregivers. That program started in 2007 and was a big win for the disability community in Kansas. At one point, I met with the then-governor Kathleen Sebelius, and the two of us had a conversation about how important it was for people with disabilities to live in the community with the support of caregivers, instead of living in nursing homes. She wholeheartedly agreed with me.

Cerebral palsy moved closer to me and seemed to be impressed.

As the years have gone by, I have learned to embrace my disability instead of fighting against it. In the winter, when the cold weather makes my spasms and stiffness worse, I stay in bed under my electric blanket about an hour longer than usual. The extra time helps me move better all day.

I don't know if cerebral palsy and memory are in any way connected, but I and several friends with cerebral palsy have talked about how we seem to have sharper memories than most other people. On various occasions, as I was talking to friends, I have been able to recall good experiences we had many years before that they had since forgotten. Seeing an unexpected smile when that happens always makes my day.

I wouldn't see the world in the same way that I do without my disability being what it is. And I also wouldn't have my service dog. I literally could not imagine my life without her. These days, cerebral palsy takes my hand, and we work together.

Today I see my disability as a buddy instead of a bully.

Late at night it still whispers, "I'll always make you different."

And I hope to God it is true.

The assignment in my creative writing class in high school was "I would hate you somewhat less if..." At the time, I wrote extensively about my cerebral palsy. But pondering the question was what began my journey to self-acceptance and what ultimately changed my attitude toward my disability.

And I am okay with where you are.

**Feeling awkward is okay.**
It's okay to be nervous around a person with a disability. Just don't stay there. Be willing to move outside of your comfort zone. You can be clumsy. That is okay, too. The only thing that will offend me is someone who will not attempt to interact with me. On the other hand, if you tell me you are nervous, I am not going to be offended in the least. In fact, it is much more likely that I am going to be impressed that you chose to be so "real" with me. And if I know that you are nervous, then I can do things that I hope will encourage you to be more comfortable with me. I can't do anything when I don't know your mindset.

**All I ask is that you try to Look Beyond.**
In the summer of 1990, I worked for a while as a counselor at a camp for children and adults with disabilities. After I had been there a few weeks, I wrote the following poem. The sentiment still rings true today.

## Look Beyond

    I might walk with a limp people notice
    Or have speech that is hard to understand
    But I can still share a smile
    Hug a friend, or hold a hand
    Maybe I was in an accident
    I could have lost my sight
    But I want to make it very clear
    The rest of me is all right
    I may have seizures sometimes
    It could be hard for me to hear
    But when you are happy, share your laughter
    And when you are sad, I'll dry your tears
    I may move very slowly
    And do some things a little different
    But that doesn't mean I want pity
    Or that I will never be content
    I like to focus on the positives
    There is so much that I can do
    The spirit inside me is able to dream
    I want that to shine through
    I accomplish goals in a unique time frame
    But they are achieved
    Some people doubt I can do it
    As for me, I believe
    Because my limitations are not that important
    They are not all that I see
    They are only a very tiny part
    Of the person who is me
    So when you first meet me, keep in mind
    Being human is our common bond
    Our lives are very different
    But to really know me, look beyond...

    We are all more the same than different.

**Thank you** for reading *More The Same Than Different: What I Wish People Knew About Respecting and Including People with Disabilities.* The idea for this book was born when one of my caregivers asked, "What simple things can people do to help you feel more empowered?"

If you have any feedback about this book, I would love to hear from you! You can contact me at morethesamethandifferent@gmail.com, and please go to Amazon and give it a review. I would sincerely appreciate it. Thanks!

**About the Author** Lorraine Cannistra was born with cerebral palsy and has spent most of her adult life learning to embrace her disability.

Chosen to represent the United States in the International Games for the Disabled in 1986 and being crowned Ms. Wheelchair Kansas in 2007 were some of the best experiences of her life, and they would never have happened if she was not a wheelchair user. Wheelchair ballroom dance is one of her passions.

As a regular blogger and nine-time contributor to the Chicken Soup for the Soul series, Lorraine enjoys telling stories to express what her life is like, with the hope of breaking down barriers between those with disabilities and those without them.

Her B.S. in English and Masters degree in Rehabilitation Counseling, as well as her vast personal experience, have uniquely prepared her for challenging some negative perceptions surrounding disability.

Lorraine can speak on a wide range of topics related to disability. Sharing information with an audience is one of Lorraines favorite things to do. Find more information and book her as a speaker at www.lorrainecannistra.com. While you're there, check out the dance videos! Her Facebook page is Lorraine Cannistra, Author, and she can be found on Twitter @LorraineCan.

Lorraine lives in Lawrence, Kansas, and shares her home with her black Lab service dog, Leah.

## Resources

National Council on Independent Living-www.ncil.org

Centers for Independent Living are full of resources and assistance for people with disabilities. There are many around the country. The NCIL website can help you find the one closest to you.

Ms. Wheelchair Kansas–mswheelchairkansas.org

Being crowned Ms. Wheelchair Kansas 2007 and holding that title for that year was one of the most empowering experiences of my life. I highly recommend it.

Ms. Wheelchair America–www.mswheelchairamerica.org

Unfortunately, not every state has a Ms. Wheelchair program yet. This site shares the history of the organization, the responsibilities of the title holder, and how people who are interested can get a program started in their state.

United Cerebral Palsy–ucp.org

There are all kinds of resources here for people of all ages who have cerebral palsy.

CARES–www.caresks.com

CARES (Canine Assistance Rehabilitation Education and Support) is the dog school where I got some additional training for my first service dog and where I got my second service dog. This organization is very near and dear to my heart.

National Alliance on Mental Illness (NAMI)–www.nami.com

This site is full of resources for people who are experiencing mental illness.

Made in United States
Orlando, FL
27 April 2023

32485167R00068